ENCOUNTERS WITH THE LIVING GOD

Old Testament Characters Tell Their Own Stories

ENCOUNTERS
with the
LIVING
GOD

ROBERT MARTIN WALKER

ABINGDON PRESS / Nashville

ENCOUNTERS WITH THE LIVING GOD:
OLD TESTAMENT CHARACTERS TELL THEIR OWN STORIES

Copyright © 2000 by Robert Martin Walker

This book is printed on acid-free paper.

Library of Congress Cataloging-in-Publication Data

Walker, Robert Martin.
    Encounters with the living God / Robert Martin Walker.
        p. cm.
    ISBN 0-687-07074-0 (alk. paper)
    1. Bible. O.T.—Biography. 2. Bible. O.T.—Devotional literature. I. Title.

BS571.W313 2000
221.9'22—dc21

99-059446

Scripture selections are from, or are adapted or paraphrased from the *New Revised Standard Version of the Bible*, copyright 1989, Division of Christian Education of the National Council of the Churches of Christ in the United States of America. Used by permission. All rights reserved.

00 01 02 03 04 05 06 07 08 09—10 9 8 7 6 5 4 3 2 1

For Patricia Jansen Walker
and
Margaret Walker Allen,

sisters by birth
who have become
sisters in faith

CONTENTS

CONTENTS

ACKNOWLEDGMENTS

J UST AS IT TAKES a village to raise a child, it takes many different people to bring a book into being.

If I were to thank all the people who had some influence on my faith, I would need an entire book to list them. Therefore, I will only mention the principal influences on this book. My professors of Old Testament helped shape my understanding of these characters and their stories: W. J. A. Powers and John Holbert of Perkins School of Theology, and Brevard Childs of Yale University Divinity School.

My immediate family has been patient and understanding throughout the process of writing. When I was their Sunday school teacher, my sons, Brandon and Matthew, allowed me to use them and their classmates as guinea pigs for some of these character portraits. My wife, Donna, has turned her keen editorial eye on this manuscript, improving it tremendously.

Finally, I am grateful to my mother and father, who told and read many of these stories to me as a child.

INTRODUCTION

A GREAT CHALLENGE FOR readers of the Bible is to enter into the drama of salvation it narrates. Our task is to discover ways that the story of God's love for the world can become our own story.

The difficulty in making the Bible's story our own is a matter of distance. The characters in the biblical drama lived many centuries ago and were part of cultures very different from ours. However, for all their differences, these people were like us in significant ways. They had dreams and disappointments, hopes and fears, moments of faith and times of unfaithfulness; in other words, they were *human*. My purpose in writing this book is to reduce the distance between us and the characters of the Old Testament, and, in so doing, to enable us to enter more fully into the biblical drama of God's love.

In order to explore the humanity of the characters of the Old Testament, we need to ask questions that the Bible doesn't directly answer. This requires us to use our imaginations. Imagination is one way to stand in the place of another person, no matter how great the distance that separates us.

What would it be like to hear Adam and Eve tell about their disobedience in the Garden of Eden? If we could hear from Cain, how would he justify the murder of his brother Abel? How would Moses describe an encounter with God on the verge of entering the Promised Land? How would Isaiah describe his call from the Lord? If we could see into the mind of Bathsheba, what would be the nature of her thoughts and feelings?

This book offers insights into questions like these. Readers are given an opportunity to explore events from the character's point of view.

Each character's story is based on the best of biblical scholarship and, at the same time, attempts to creatively capture the character's unique voice. What finally emerges from these portraits is a picture of God through the eyes of Old Testament characters.

The characters of the Old Testament have fascinating tales to tell! There are stories of love and hatred, victory and defeat, joy and despair, faithfulness and disobedience, delight and misery. Above all, these stories are deeply human: They narrate the heights of joy and love, as well as the depths of sin and evil.

These stories also describe encounters with God; and these encounters are not always pleasant. Adam and Eve are reprimanded and sent away from Eden. Abraham is commanded to sacrifice his son, Isaac. Moses is told that he cannot cross the River Jordan and enter into the Promised Land. Job, in agony, cries out, "Why me, Lord?" Yet even when these divine encounters are difficult, the reality of God's grace emerges.

I have used the first-person voice in an attempt to breathe life into the characters of the Old Testament. I hope that you, the reader, will see them as thinking, feeling, acting humans who are much like you and me. In this way, the possibility of seeing ourselves in their stories opens up.

In my earlier book, *The Jesus I Knew: Creative Portrayals of Gospel Characters* (Abingdon Press, 1996), my goal was to bring to life characters who knew Jesus. I hope this book will do the same with characters who knew, and were known by, God.

Entering into the stories of these characters will engage your imagination. Although I've done some of the work for you by putting myself into the mind of the characters, using your own imagination will only deepen your insights into who these people were, and who God is. For, ultimately, God plays the lead role in the biblical drama of salvation.

With each character, I have indicated relevant passages of Scripture on which that character's portrait is based. Some of these passages are quite lengthy, covering an entire book of the Bible (such as with Jeremiah and Esther). Reading the Scripture will give you the vital information you need in order to get the fullest sense of each character as a person—as a human being—through the portraits presented here.

My hope is that by entering into the world of the Bible, you will not only be able to better grasp who the characters are, but you will more fully understand who *you* are in relation to God.

—Robert Martin Walker

I
BEGINNINGS

Adam and Eve

Read Genesis 3.

Adam

EVEN AS I SPOKE, shame and guilt began washing over me like rain. In the cool of the evening, when the Lord asked me if I had eaten of the forbidden Tree, I pointed a finger of accusation at Eve.

"The woman whom you gave to be with me," I said, "she offered me fruit from the tree, and I ate."

And, yes, these words placed blame not only on Eve for giving me the fruit, but also on the Lord for creating her. Never had I spoken such hateful and false words. This second sin was as wicked as the first.

How could I have betrayed my beloved Eve? She was the one who transformed my life from an "I" to a "We." Before Eve, I was alone, having only animals for companionship. I was empty and incomplete, longing for something I couldn't imagine. The Lord was with me. But loving the Lord isn't the same as loving a living, breathing woman with warmth and passion. The Lord is like a Father. Eve—well, Eve is a part of me and I am a part of her. We are one flesh, and, because we are one, our lives are forever entwined.

Before eating the fruit, we lived in pure innocence, having no worries and no fears. We were blissfully ignorant of our nakedness. We knew no sin, no guilt, and no shame before the fruit of the Tree opened our eyes. Neither did we know pain, toil, or danger.

After eating the fruit, we were ashamed to face the Lord. We felt guilty and foolishly thought we could hide from our Creator. (With the Lord, there is no place to hide.) Our garments woven from leaves couldn't conceal the truth that we had sinned against the Lord.

Now that my eyes have been opened, I realize that we can never return to the paradise of Eden. Sin has consequences. A relationship may be healed if broken, but life does not go on as before.

Thus, Eve must have pain in childbirth, and I must toil and labor to live. This is the way it must be, says the Lord. I came from dust, and now my survival—as well as Eve's—depends on bringing forth crops from the dust.

And yet even despite our sin, despite our failure to obey and follow the Lord's command, despite our self-chosen separation from him, the Lord did not abandon us. He made clothes for us from animal skins, and he dressed us.

Now that my eyes have been opened, I more clearly understand the choice I made by eating the fruit. When Eve ate the fruit, something in her changed. Her eyes reflected the knowledge of good and evil. Her innocence had been swallowed in that first bite.

I now see that to not eat would have meant a life without Eve. Oh, we might have existed together, but not as partners. She would have looked upon me as a mother would an innocent child. I want to be a husband, not a child.

So I ate, and in eating I made my choice. I chose Eve over obedience to the Lord. I chose companionship over compliance. I know it was wrong, but I could not bear the thought of losing what had become most precious to me.

We are exiled from paradise now. A flaming sword bars the way back. But I would not go back, even if I could, now that my eyes have been opened. Once lost, innocence cannot be regained. Now, good and evil are daily decisions. In Eden, there was only one choice: whether or not to eat of the sacred Tree. East of Eden, every day is filled with choices.

Even though I must work and sweat to grow crops and make a living from the soil, I somehow feel a sense of freedom. Although the work is hard, I find satisfaction in providing for my family. Eden was paradise, but perhaps things were bound to work out this way after all.

Eve and I will create a new life together in this dangerous place. It will be a hard life, but it will be a *shared* life. Eve and I will live together, work together, create children together. I can bear the burdens we will face, as long as Eve is with me.

We no longer have paradise, but we have each other. And I know that the Lord will be with us, no matter where we live.

Eve

I *despise* that serpent who lured me to eat of the forbidden Tree. If I ever see him again, I will grind his head under my heel. Oh, the pleasure it would give me to crush his flesh into the dirt! If I hadn't listened to the serpent, we would still be in Eden.

Already I miss the lush, green trees and the lovely, fragrant flowers of Eden. Adam and I were so completely happy in that beautiful garden, laughing and frolicking and playing. What a joy it was to awake in the morning to a new day of exploring. Each day was filled with adventure and fresh discoveries. Even more remarkable, in Eden there was no toiling for food, no danger from wild beasts, and no pain.

But the serpent's lies ruined it all. He made the fruit seem so inviting that it practically called out, *Taste me*. When I mentioned that eating the fruit of this particular tree was forbidden by the Lord, the serpent scoffed, "When you eat of the fruit, you will be like God, knowing good and evil."

At that time, I didn't even know the meaning of the words *good* and *evil*. But I wanted to know. Even more, I wanted to be like the Lord, who seemed so much wiser than I or Adam. Was it wrong to want to be like our Creator? If the Lord didn't want us to eat of the sacred Tree, why was it put there in the garden in the first place? Did the Lord realize how curious we were?

I so very much wanted to know good and evil, and the fruit seemed so desirable, I plucked a piece off the tree and ate. Then I gave some to Adam, who also ate. I know it was selfish to involve Adam in my disobedience. But whatever our fate, I wanted us to face it together.

Immediately, we both realized we had done something very wrong. Knowing good and evil for the first time, we saw our nakedness and were ashamed. I felt exposed and vulnerable. Adam and I quickly sewed leaves together to cover ourselves. And then we hid ourselves from the Lord. How foolish of us! Imagine the absurdity of our thinking we could hide from our Creator, the One who made us.

When the Lord found us, he questioned Adam first. I was hurt when Adam blamed me for giving him the fruit (even though I had). However, when the Lord questioned me next, I did a similar thing, accusing the serpent of trickery. There was plenty of blame to share; each of us was responsible for making the wrong choices.

Our disobedience has consequences. Not only must we say good-bye to paradise, now we will lead more difficult lives. Work will eclipse play. Pain will be mixed with pleasure. Danger will stalk us. Our lives will be lived outside the comfort of Eden.

Yet, while paradise is lost to us, Adam and I still have each other. We are one flesh—each a part of the other—and we will work to make a new life together. We will share in the tasks of providing our food, clothing, and shelter, and raising children. Life will be harder, yet it can also be satisfying.

Now that our eyes are opened to the knowledge of good and evil, we are no longer innocent; such knowledge comes with a cost. Although we can't go back to the paradise of Eden, we can go forward into the world. The Lord not only created Eden, but the rest of the earth as well. And we know that the Lord is present not only in Eden, but everywhere outside Eden.

I take comfort knowing that I will be with my husband, Adam, in our new life. With him by my side, I can face whatever the future holds. In some strange way, I find the idea of this new life exciting. East of Eden, there are risks and dangers. We are traveling into the unknown, charged with the task of creating our own garden out of a wilderness. Were it not for Adam, I would be trembling with fear.

I cannot go back to Eden, even if the thought of it seems inviting. Now that I know about good and evil, I am responsible for my choices; *each* of us will be. We must contend with the consequences of choosing evil and the rewards of choosing what is good and right. This freedom to choose is both a burden and a gift. But I cannot see how it could be otherwise. Perhaps the Lord had a certain purpose for putting the sacred Tree in the center of the garden.

Dear Lord, I thank you for the knowledge of good and evil and for the freedom to choose. Help me to choose what is right and good, that I may obey your will. Give me the courage to repent of the evil I have chosen. In your holy name I pray. Amen.

Questions for Reflection and Discussion

• How do Adam and Eve feel about each other? In what ways do they express their love for each other? How does their love lead to disobedience to God? What sacrifices have you made for those whom you love?

• Is Eve to blame for Adam's eating the forbidden fruit? Why or why not? What are some other possible reasons for Adam's disobedience? When have you tried to rationalize doing something wrong?

• Why do Adam and Eve try to hide from God? What makes them recognize their nakedness and vu lnerability? Is God's punishment of them just? What does this story say about our condition as humans? Where are you in this story?

Cain

Read Genesis 4:1-16.

NIGHTS ARE THE MOST difficult times to endure. With effort I can struggle through days. During the day there is light and movement. I can distract myself from the memories that torment my dreams. As I walk in the light of day, I can focus on things around me: a bird's song, drifting clouds, my aching feet, the wind on my face. I can lose myself in the tasks and routines of daytime.

After sunset, darkness descends, and with the dark comes the cold sweat of fear and guilt. In the vast darkness, memories of my sin plague me. There are no diversions to occupy my mind; I am haunted by thoughts that keep me from sleeping. When I finally drift into a fitful slumber, the nightmares come.

The nightmare I've been having lately is the worst so far. I am walking in a freshly tilled field under a sunny sky, sowing seeds in the furrows. Suddenly, the sky turns black as if a storm were approaching. The seeds lying on the ground turn into drops of blood, making the field blood-red all around me. And then I hear voices, hundreds of voices—as if the seeds were screaming. "*Murderer—murderer—murderer,*" the voices chant, louder and louder. I cover my ears to shut out the awful noise, but the voices screech inside my head and cannot be silenced. "*MURDERER! MURDERER!*" they keep screaming. And then I awaken, afraid to sleep again lest the nightmare return.

The accusing voices from my dream speak the truth. I am a murderer. Worse, I am the murderer of my own brother. The memory of my sin is almost too much to bear. I often wish that the Lord would strike me down so that I could join Abel. That fate would be easier than wandering through the countryside alone and forsaken, without the comfort of family or friends, laboring under a crushing weight of sin and guilt.

I have asked the question thousands of times: Why was my offering rejected by the Lord, while Abel's was praised? Is the Lord arbitrary in his praising and cursing? Does he simply prefer the fat of animals over the fruit of the earth? Or was there something in the way I presented my offering to the Lord that invited rejection?

Yes, there must have been something I said or did that wasn't right. I've searched my memory countless times to recall my attitude when I made the offering. But everything is blurry, like a mirage. I can't remember whether I was angry or calm, whether I was eager or reluctant, whether I was reverent or arrogant. "What is the 'right' attitude to accompany an offering?" I ask myself aloud.

I went through the ritual movements of the offering with efficiency. I piled the grains and fruits on the stone altar. Then I ignited the wood underneath. I lifted up my hands to the Lord and spoke the proper words of thanksgiving. Why wasn't that enough to please the Lord? What more did the Lord require of me?

One thing I remember clearly. I remember being in a hurry to gather the grains and fruits for the offering. You see, the harvest had already started, and I had so little time to collect the offering. Maybe I skimped a little on the quality of the ears of corn. I might have picked a few apples up off the ground rather than plucking them fresh from the tree. And yes, in my haste, I could have gathered some ears of grain that were not as full as the others.

But Abel had the luxury of time to make his offering. There were only a few ewes giving birth in his small flock. He took great care to find a firstborn lamb without blemish. He could afford to take time because he wasn't under the pressure of harvesting the grain before the rains came and destroyed a season's work.

I admit to being angry with Abel. The Lord's praise of Abel's offering made my offering seem all the more unworthy. Abel, my younger brother, was trying to show me up, just as he always did. He was perfect in too many ways. He was the perfect son, the perfect brother, the perfect worshiper. When measured against Abel's standard, I never measured up.

The Lord knew I was angry. As I stormed away from the altars, he warned me that sin was lurking near and I must master my desires or succumb to them. If the Lord knew I was angry, why didn't I receive more than a mere warning? Why didn't the Lord send me away so my rage could cool? But that isn't the Lord's way.

When I lured Abel into the field and murdered him with a stone, anger had blinded me to what I was doing. I wanted only to kill Abel's perfection. Instead, I killed my brother. Immediately, I was horrified over what I had done. I dug a shallow grave and covered his body with dirt. I devised a story to tell about how he had wandered into the wilderness in search of a lost sheep.

But the Lord is not so easily fooled. When the Lord asked me the whereabouts of my brother, he already knew. My answer haunts me. "Am I my brother's keeper?" I said, hoping to deflect the Lord's scrutiny of me. But the Lord knew the truth. My brother's blood had cried out to the Lord from the ground. There was bitter irony in this: The very soil that I had so carefully tilled betrayed me.

My punishment was exile from the land I loved. I loved my precious land above all else. Never was I happier than when I felt the moist, loamy dirt in my fingers. I relished the exhausting toil of plowing fields. I cherished the elegance of sowing seeds. I rejoiced in the miracle of growth of crops. The land sustained us; it provided crops to feed us, and grass to feed sheep and cattle. Without my land, I was nothing.

Exile meant that I was a fugitive. As a fugitive, I would be tracked down and killed! I begged the Lord to lessen this punishment. Wasn't losing my beloved land harsh enough? Living in constant fear of death was more than I could endure.

But the Lord, who is just, is also merciful. The Lord placed upon me a mark of his protection. Everyone who saw this sign kept their distance from me. They knew they would be punished sevenfold if they killed me. Thus, even this protective sign became a curse, because it isolated me from people.

I am alive, but my life is a living death. Everything I have loved is now lost to me. Never again can I see my family. I will never again feast my eyes on the beautiful fields of Canaan. I feel far away from the Lord's presence. I am condemned to wander aimlessly, plagued by thoughts of what might have been.

Remorse possesses my thoughts. Peace is not to be found, even in sleep. The question I asked the Lord in fear and anger echoes in my mind: *Am I my brother's keeper?* This question offered as a defense now condemns me. I know the truth. I *am* my brother's keeper. Or, rather, I *should* have been my brother's keeper. I could have hated Abel's perfect offering, but loved him. Now that he's gone—and by my own hand—I realize my love for him. Abel was only doing his best—something I seldom did.

I am finally the *best* at something. I am the world's best sufferer. Protected by the Lord's sign, I must live out my days in infamy. If I could go back, do things over again, I would take more time and care in my offering to the Lord. If I could do it over again, I would hold my temper, and the Lord might let me keep my land. If only I could do it over again.

O Lord, let me be remorseful when I have sinned. Use this remorse to make me confess my sin and ask for your forgiveness. Give me the strength and courage to face the consequences of my sin. In your name I pray. Amen.

Questions for Reflection and Discussion

• What are your feelings toward Cain as he tells his story? Do you accept his explanation of how he came to murder Abel? At what points do you identify with his tragic tale?

• What was Cain's attitude in gathering his offering? Why was Cain's offering rejected while Abel's was accepted? When have you approached the Lord with a wrong attitude?

• Is Cain's punishment just? How is his punishment merciful? How is his punishment painful? When have you had to endure consequences of wrong actions?

Noah

Read Genesis 7–9.

WHEN THE LORD TOLD me to build an ark, I tried not to show my surprise. *Why in the world would I need an ark on dry land?* I asked myself. The nearest water was many miles away. I also wondered—silently, of course—*How will my family and neighbors react to such a strange event? I will become the laughingstock of Canaan!*

Then the Lord gave me the dimensions of the ark my sons and I were to build. It would be a massive vessel with three decks, capable of carrying a vast amount of cargo! I wondered, *What will such a huge ship carry?* My question was soon answered. The Lord instructed me to take the male and female of every creature that populated the earth! I was dying to ask the Lord the purpose for this when the Lord again spoke to me.

The Lord said, "I have decided to destroy the creatures I created, for they have become wicked, violent, and corrupt. Only those aboard the ark will be saved."

Although I did not speak, I was filled with questions about what the Lord had told me. *Was such a radical cleansing of the earth necessary? While destroying all living things could be an act of justice, was it an act of love? Didn't the Lord's creatures deserve a final chance to repent?*

Since these questions were unanswerable, except by the Lord, I pondered practical matters. *How could I build such an enormous ark? How could we possibly collect so many creatures? Could my family and I survive aboard a floating vessel with so many animals? Why were we chosen to survive when so many others would perish?*

These questions and many others raced through my mind after the Lord spoke to me; but I did not ask even a single one of them. I am merely a man, a mortal, a creature. It is not my place to question the ways of Almighty God. God's wisdom is as far above my wisdom as the stars are above the ground. A sheep doesn't question its shepherd, but rather follows him.

I must admit, however, I was overwhelmed by this astonishing encounter with the Lord. It took me years afterward to assimilate all that had been told me in those few moments. Yet I obeyed, even though I did not understand the reasons for the Lord's action. To disobey would have been unthinkable.

First, I gathered my family around the evening fire to make known to them what the Lord had said to me. As the patriarch of the family, I knew that my authority would not be questioned—at least not aloud. My wife and I had raised Shem, Ham, and Japheth well, and we had chosen good, faithful wives for them. They would believe their father, and obey. Even so, I was anxious about telling my family what the Lord had commanded.

My apprehension over speaking to my family was due to the enormous task facing us. Not only were we commanded to build a gigantic, multidecked vessel, we were to fill it with thousands of animals, birds, and insects! And not only this, we were to take enough food to feed ourselves and the animals for many weeks. How could eight men and women accomplish such an awesome feat?

As expected, my wife, sons, and daughters-in-law did not oppose my word from the Lord. There were some raised eyebrows and a few glances exchanged between my sons and their wives, but no objections were voiced. They too seemed more concerned by the mountain of work that lay ahead. After a time of silence, we started planning how to accomplish the task the Lord had set before us.

Fortunately, I was able to hire a cadre of workers to help us build the ark. Although they wondered aloud what crazy man would build such a massive ship so far from water, they were happy to receive their wages.

My initial fear about my neighbors' reactions was well founded. Each day while we worked on the ark, the neighbors and other onlookers gathered nearby and mocked us. "Why are you building a boat, Noah? Do you plan on sailing the desert?" one of them yelled. Eventually, they began to refer to my ark as "Noah's Land Ship." By the tone of their insults, I could tell they thought I was insane. At times, I wondered whether they were right! The Lord did not come to me again until the ark was built.

When the ark was finished and we started loading it with creatures of every kind, the scoffers were even more delighted. They hooted and howled at our efforts to get the wild beasts up the ship's ramp. They started calling the boat "Noah's Zoo." Their scornful laughter dogged our every step.

When the rains started, I felt pity for my tormentors. For the first few days, they stubbornly stood in the rain, yelling insults at us. But as the rains continued and the waters rose, the people outside the ark stopped their jeering and taunting. Realizing they were in trouble, they now begged for passage aboard "Noah's Zoo." As the rains continued, their pleas were drowned out by the noise of thunder and squalls. Every one of them would soon perish in the Great Flood.

Life aboard the ark was an ordeal. Although we had stockpiled a massive amount of food, after feeding the creatures on board we were nearly too exhausted to eat. And the putrid stench of so many animals caused us to choke down our bread! Once we were afloat, the wind and waves made us seasick. A few of the larger animals became ill. Life on the ark tested our faith in the Lord and our goodwill toward one another. Many times, I had to hold my temper when one of my sons complained.

The trials of our weeks on the ark were not only bodily, but spiritual. We grieved for the poor souls destroyed by the flood. All of us had friends and relatives among the drowned. Shem, in particular, was devastated by the loss of his best friend, Tabor. Our nights were tormented by visions of rising waters and drowning people. As the waters rose, remaining survivors outside the ark scrambled to higher ground. Within days, people were fighting one another for the shrinking land on the mountaintops. Brother fought against brother for survival. Chaos erupted as the land vanished under water. Corpses emerged all around us, bumping against the ark. I was grateful when these reminders of death disappeared again beneath the roiling waters.

After forty days of a constant deluge, the rain suddenly stopped. The world had become a giant ocean; and other than the scant floating wreckage of civilization, ours was the only vessel floating upon it. When the sun appeared, we gathered on the top deck and sang songs of praise to the Lord for delivering us. Yet we would not see dry land for many weeks to come.

I was impatient to discover if the waters had subsided enough to land our ark. I sent out a dove, but it returned after a few days. Another week passed and I sent the dove out again. It returned after a few days with a fresh olive leaf in its beak! We all sent up a shout of joy: There was dry land somewhere!

Of course, it took months before the land was dry enough to walk on. At first, everything was a sea of mud. But the sun and wind worked their miracles, and the earth slowly began to resume its pre-Flood form.

My first act after leaving the boat was to build an altar and offer a sacrifice of thanksgiving to the Lord. The Lord's presence came near the altar and, again, the Lord addressed me. "Be fruitful and multiply," said the Lord.

My sons will have no problem obeying this command, I thought silently.

Then the Lord answered a question that had distressed me during my months on the ark. *Could this ever happen again?* The destruction of life, human and otherwise, had weighed heavily on my heart. I understood the Lord's disgust and anger with humanity. Violence and corruption had replaced love and obedience to the Lord in the hearts of men. I understood why the Lord wanted to start over.

My heart, however, was troubled by the destruction. Surely some innocent souls had been annihilated along with the masses of the guilty. Corruption had not infected every person.

But the Lord reassured me. "I establish my covenant with you," said the Lord, "that never again shall all flesh be cut off by the waters of a flood, and never again shall there be a flood to destroy the earth."

Then the Lord created a sign of his covenant: a bow of colors arced across the sky. Never had I seen anything so radiant and resplendent! The bow was majestic and dazzling. My family and I feasted our eyes on the Lord's sign, overjoyed at what it meant for future generations.

We didn't view the rainbow for long. There was much work to be done. Building an ark is a difficult enough undertaking; imagine the challenge of rebuilding a civilization!

Dear Lord, may I follow the example of Noah, who obeyed you even when he didn't understand the reasons for your commands. Grant me the deep trust and abiding loyalty Noah demonstrated. I pray this in your name. Amen.

Questions for Reflection and Discussion

• What would have been your reaction if the Lord had told you to build an ark? In what ways do you identify with Noah's questions about the Lord's command? When have you felt called to attempt an "impossible" task due to your faith?

• What enables Noah to obey even when he doesn't fully understand or agree with the reasons for the Lord's actions? What difficulties do Noah and his family face once the ark is afloat? What enables you to persevere in difficult circumstances?

• Why are Noah's feelings ambivalent about the Great Flood? How can you identify with his sadness over the loss of life? How is God's covenant with Noah (and with all of creation) an act of love? In your personal experience, what are the signs of God's love?

Sarah

Read Genesis 15–18.

WHEN THE LORD ACCUSED me of laughing, I denied it out of shame and fear. But the Lord spoke the truth. I *did* laugh.

You would have laughed too if you had suffered decades of humiliation over being childless. During my "child-bearing years" (why do I still call them this?), I was plagued by the shame of barrenness. Nobody ever mentioned it—they feared what Abraham would do to them—but I heard their silence. I could read the scorn in their eyes. I could feel the looks of pity cast in my direction. And although no one ever said it to my face, I knew my nickname: Barren Sarah.

All around me, mothers were cuddling babies in their arms. Each kiss planted on a child was like a dagger in my heart. Oh, I played the role of doting Aunt Sarah very well. Children loved me for the attention I gave them, and mothers appreciated relief from the constant task of caring for their children. To them I appeared to be a happy caregiver. But my heart was breaking.

And while I was heartsick for myself, my heart hurt even more for Abraham. He wanted an heir so badly! He even dreamed of our having a child. He confided in me that the Lord had promised to make him the father of a great nation, with descendants as countless as the stars. I couldn't fathom what seemed to be such an absurd idea; I would have been content just to have *one* son to carry on our lineage.

I wanted so badly to believe Abraham's dreams of a child that I allowed myself to hope they might be true. But when, year after long year, I still had not conceived, I gave up hope that I would ever be able to bear a child for my husband.

That's when I told Abraham of my plan. I determined that the only way he would have an heir would be for him to have a child with another woman. As much as it pained me to think of it, I told Abraham to lie with our slave girl, Hagar. This, at least, would allow my husband's bloodline to survive.

At first, Abraham was reluctant. But finally, he gave in to my wishes. Hagar became pregnant immediately, as if to emphasize my lack of fertility. She wore her pregnancy like a new tunic, glowing with pride at the swelling of her belly. Soon, she was acting as though *she* was the mistress of the house and I was the slave. "Bring me that jar of water, Sarah. I'm too heavy to move!" she said.

It was difficult enough to endure the knowledge that Hagar was carrying my husband's child. But her superior manner was unbearable. I told Abraham to discipline her, but he refused to become involved, telling me, "Do with her what you please." What pleased me was to punish her for a contemptuous attitude. So I gave Hagar more chores than she could possibly accomplish in the hours of the day. I assigned her the most miserable tasks: cleaning out the stable, butchering the cattle, emptying the waste jars. I was secretly relieved when she fled into the wilderness, although Abraham was beside himself with worry. After all, she was carrying his heir.

Hagar eventually returned, but as a different person. She politely submitted to me and served me as a daughter would a mother. I forgave her earlier slights and was midwife to the birth of Abraham's son, Ishmael.

Now that Abraham had a son, I was relieved of my obligation to produce one. Yet Abraham held on to his dream. One day, he told me of yet another vision in which the Lord appeared. In this dream, the Lord told him that Ishmael would not be his heir, but that Abraham and I would be parents of a son!

This time, I was incredulous! Imagine the absurdity of two people of our advanced years having a child. Abraham sheepishly admitted that he had even laughed at the thought. But the Lord reassured him of its truth.

Soon after this last vision, three strangers came to Mamre, where we were encamped in a grove of tall oaks. When these travelers appeared suddenly, Abraham sprang into action. He offered them hospitality (for which he was renowned), even attending them while they took refreshment. I hurriedly made some cakes for them. I then stayed in our tent, as was the custom; women were supposed to keep out of sight while the men were dining. But I hovered close to the tent door so I could hear their conversation.

Suddenly, I heard one of the strangers speak in a peculiar tone of voice. The voice said, "I will return to you in nine months, and you will have a son."

Hearing this, I couldn't keep silence. After so many years of desperate yearning for a child, it was as if whatever was holding back the laughter and tears shattered within me. I began to laugh and cry at the same time. I tried to hold the laughter in, but it was overwhelming. The thought of an old man and an old woman having a baby was crazy. I had gone through the change of life decades before. What kind of divine joke was this?

Some of my laughter was provoked by the idea of physical passion being rekindled between Abraham and me at our age. But there was a darker side to my laughter as well—it was laced with bitterness. I had been disappointed by the Lord's promise two times already. I had stopped believing in my husband's reassuring dreams. In my laughter, scorn was woven with hilarity.

The force of my laughter knocked me off my feet, and I lay writhing on the ground like a beetle on its back. I couldn't catch my breath enough to stand up, so I lay on the floor of the tent, helpless.

I heard the Lord ask Abraham, "Why did Sarah laugh? Is anything too wonderful for the Lord?" Of course, the Lord, who knows all things, knew the answer. Nevertheless, I denied it out of fear and shame. "I did not laugh," I lied. I was afraid to confess my laughter because it was the laughter of disbelief.

Over the next nine months, a miracle occurred, just as the Lord had promised: A child of hope grew within me. I shared in the miracle of motherhood. Every morning I would awake and feel my swollen belly, making sure that I wasn't in one of Abraham's dreams. I met each new day with the joyful knowledge that I was going to be a mother. And not only a mother, but the mother of a very special child. As it turned out, the divine joke was on me!

When our son was born, there was no doubt in my mind as to what his name should be. Abraham and I agreed that he should be called

Isaac, which means "laughter." At Isaac's birth, I laughed again. This time, my laughter was pure and true, without bitterness or rancor; for God had given us the promised child, whose birth was a wellspring of unending joy and a source of grateful laughter.

Almighty God, help me to believe your promises even when they seem distant and uncertain. May hope be born in me, as it was in Sarah. Make my laughter strong and pure, so that it expresses joy rather than scorn. I pray this in your holy name. Amen.

Questions for Reflection and Discussion

• Imagine yourself in Sarah's situation. How might you have coped with years of desperately wanting to have a child and not being able to do so? Sarah experiences humiliation from others over her circumstances. When have you been in a situation, beyond your control, where you similarly experienced pain or humiliation?

• If you were Sarah, would you have believed in Abraham's dreams of having a son? Why or why not? What enables you to believe the word of another person?

• Describe the two different kinds of laughter that Sarah experiences (first at Mamre, and later at Isaac's birth). What causes scornful laughter in you? What causes joyful laughter? How can laughter be an expression of both faith and disbelief?

Abraham

Read Genesis 17:1-8; 21:2-3; 22:1-19.

WHEN MY BELOVED SON, Isaac, was a boy, the Lord came to me in a vision. Throughout my life, the Lord has spoken to me in visions and dreams. This time, my encounter with the Lord was more like a nightmare. After the Lord called my name I said, "Here I am."

Then came the Lord's instructions. "Take your only son, Isaac, whom you love, and go to the land of Moriah, and offer him there as a sacrifice. I will show you the mountain on which to build an altar."

When I awoke from this vision, questions overwhelmed me. *Why would the Lord command such a thing? Did the Lord not remember the agonizing years Sarah and I waited for Isaac's miraculous arrival? How could the Lord order me to take the life of this Child of Promise, the one through whom the Lord's covenant would be fulfilled? Why was I being told to cut the throat of the Promise and consume it in flames? If the Lord needed a life, why couldn't he take mine instead of my son's?*

Inwardly, I was in agony over what the Lord had commanded me to do. I felt as if my heart were being ripped, still beating, from my chest. Never had I labored under such a crushing weight.

But outwardly, I was calm. I tried to appear normal so that Sarah, a born worrier, wouldn't be anxious about my task. I explained to Sarah that the Lord had commanded me to journey to Moriah to offer a sacrifice, but I couldn't bring myself to tell her who the sacrifice would be. When I told her that Isaac would accompany me, I thought my resolve would falter; but it didn't. Being a protective mother, Sarah argued that Isaac was too young for such a journey. Going against every fatherly instinct within me, I convinced her that Isaac would be safe.

As my two servants and I cut wood for the offering, I winced at each blow of the ax, imagining it falling on my beloved son's neck. But I hid my turmoil from Sarah and Isaac—especially Isaac. I wanted his death to be painless; the anticipation of death only deepens the pain.

The three-day journey to the wilderness of Moriah was a death march. I couldn't eat. I slept little. I drank only enough water to keep myself alive. I couldn't bear to look upon my beloved Isaac, who was excited about his first journey into the wilderness. He had no idea this was to be his last.

As the jagged mountains appeared on the horizon, a great sadness gripped me. Isaac would never know the joys and challenges of growing to manhood. He would never marry and have children, never look with favor upon a grandchild—nor would *I* know any grandchildren. I grieved the loss of Isaac's future, and my own. Without him, Sarah and I would have no descendants, and our lineage would die with us.

I wondered if I had offended the Lord in some way. I searched my past for sins against the Lord and found many. One night on the journey, I slipped away from our camp after dark and made a guilt-offering to the Lord. I prayed to the Lord, asking the question that was tormenting me: "WHY?" But the Lord was silent.

Wasn't there any other way to satisfy the Lord? I knew that the Lord's ways were beyond my understanding. But is the Lord only satisfied by blind obedience from his creatures? Surely the same Lord who had blessed an old man and woman with the infant son they never thought they could have is also a Lord who is merciful and abounding in steadfast love! If I were to lose my son, how could I go on?

We arrive at our final destination. Leaving the two servants at the foot of the mountain, Isaac and I begin our ascent. We also leave the ass and carry the wood on our backs. Each step I take draws me nearer to the moment of sacrifice, the moment of death. I feel as if the wood on my back is made of stone.

After hours of effort, we arrive at the place where the altar is to be built. Isaac is eager to help carry the stones that will compose the altar's base. I work slowly, feeling my age. Shortly, the altar is built and the wood piled underneath.

In pure innocence, Isaac asks a question that rends my heart: "Father, where is the lamb for the offering?"

I can't think of anything to say, except, "The Lord will provide the lamb, my son." *My son is the lamb!*

Isaac doesn't speak or struggle when I bind his hands. I can barely tie the knots, my hands are shaking so badly. When I tie the cloth around his mouth, I see the trust in his eyes, and I tremble. I cannot look into those eyes if I am to do this. I lay him on the altar and raise the knife high, poised for the death blow. I must do this quickly or courage will fail me. I close my eyes, squeezing out tears that drop onto Isaac.

"Abraham! Abraham!" a voice interrupts. *It is the voice of the Lord!* "Do not lay your hand on the boy or do anything to him." Hearing these words, I drop the knife. It clangs against the altar rocks. "For now I know that you fear me, since you have not withheld your beloved son, your only son, from me."

I collapse on the altar against Isaac, wrapping my arms around him. I cannot speak. He is covered with my tears. I look into his eyes, and he is crying too. Does he understand what has just happened?

Suddenly, I see a ram, caught in a nearby thicket by its horns. Yes, the Lord *has* provided, just as I told Isaac! Will this affirm my son's trust in me? Have I lost his trust?

I unbind Isaac, fearing that he will run away and never return. Instead, he wraps his arms around me and grips me tightly, as if he will never let go; neither do I want to let go. Finally, the bleating of the ram demands my attention, and I arise with my son.

I slash the throat of the ram, overjoyed that it has taken Isaac's place on the altar. As the fire consumes the ram, I think to myself that never before has the aroma of an offering been so delightful.

Then, the Lord speaks again. "Because you have obeyed me, I will make your offspring as many as the stars in the sky and the sands on the seashore. And your offspring shall triumph over their enemies. By your offspring all the nations of the earth shall be blessed." I don't think Isaac can hear the voice of the Lord, but someday—when he is of age—I will explain everything to him.

The sun is low on the horizon as the last embers of the fire die out. Isaac and I descend the mountain in silence. Words elude me as I lay my arm across his small shoulders. This gesture says what I cannot: I love you. The Child of Promise has been saved, and the Lord's promise to me will be kept. But at this moment, I have only one thought: My beloved son, Isaac, is alive!

Almighty God, grant me the steadfast faith of Abraham, who trusted you to fulfill your promises. Help me to obey you even when I don't understand the reasons for your command. Help me to trust in your love and mercy, especially when there seem to be reasons to doubt them. In your name I pray. Amen.

Questions for Reflection and Discussion

• If you were Abraham, what questions would you have had about God's command to sacrifice Isaac? Why does Abraham keep God's command a secret from Sarah and Isaac? When has God called you to perform a difficult task?

• What thoughts might have been racing through Abraham's mind as he approached the place of sacrifice? What inner struggle does Abraham engage in as he prepares Isaac for sacrifice? What aspects of obeying God cause struggles within you?

• What emotions do you think Abraham feels when God tells him not to harm his son? What thoughts might have been going through Isaac's mind? How does Isaac's "rescue" allow God's covenant with Abraham to be fulfilled? What does this story say about the nature of God's love?

Jacob and Esau

Read Genesis 25–35.

Esau: Jacob, it's time we sat down together and said what's in our hearts. There are many wounds between us that need to be healed.

Jacob: I agree. It is time we had an honest talk. I'm sure you have many things you want to say to me.

Esau: It's amazing I'm even *speaking* to you after the malicious things you did to me when we were younger.

Jacob: You are right. I was a scoundrel. But you should have been on your guard! You knew how Mother could scheme on my behalf. She doted on me, probably because you were Father's favorite.

Esau: Well, you stole my birthright! That had nothing to do with Mother.

Jacob: You shouldn't have traded your firstborn rights away for a bowl of stew. Anyone who would do such a thing doesn't deserve his birthright.

Esau: I was *famished*. What good is a birthright if you're dead from starvation? You took advantage of me. That's when I realized why you were named Jacob: You *grab* for everything you can get.

Jacob: I was selfish and immature in my youth. I grew up—eventually. And so did you.

Esau: Youth? We were *forty years old* when you stole Father's blessing!

Have you forgotten your own devious plot, which you and Mother devised? You dressed in my clothes and put sheep's fur on your hands and neck to fool our poor, old, blind father. It was bad enough, stealing from your twin brother; but deceiving a dying blind man is about as low as you can get. He gave you the power of his blessing, and I was cheated again!

Jacob: That ruse was Mother's idea. She even said she'd take the blame if Father wasn't fooled and cursed me. I just went along with what she wanted.

Esau: You were a willing accomplice, grabbing again for what was mine. I wanted to kill you!

Jacob: And I ran away like a scared lamb. Actually, Mother sent me away to stay with our Uncle Laban. You'll be pleased to know that I got what was coming to me there. I worked for seven years to earn the right to marry his younger daughter, Rachel. But Laban tricked me into marrying Rachel's older sister, Leah, instead. Then I had to work *another* seven years for the right to marry Rachel, my true love!

Esau: Well, you did end your servitude with Uncle Laban a wealthy man. And I heard how you did it. You cleverly cut a deal to keep only the spotted sheep for yourself. Then, you put striped reeds in front of the troughs, where the sheep mated, knowing that their offspring would be spotted! You grabbed what wasn't yours once again.

Jacob: Well, he deserved it! He was trying to send me away with barely enough to keep my family alive. Laban was a wily old codger. When we parted, we built a memorial out of stones and pledged never to cross into each other's territory. Although I didn't care if I ever saw him again, I did feel a little guilty taking his daughters and grandchildren so far away.

Esau: You're such a coward, Jacob. Do you remember what happened when you and I met again, twenty years after the "blessing theft"? You used your wives and children as an escort to win my sympathy. You were so afraid that I'd kill you. Didn't you know I couldn't keep the fires of rage burning against my twin brother for so long?

Jacob: I was afraid—and with good reason. The night before we met, something eerie happened at Peniel, something that affected me deeply. A stranger came to me, as if in a dream, and we wrestled until dawn. Neither of us could get the better of the other until he used a strange power to dislocate my hip. But still I wouldn't let him go until he gave me a blessing.

Esau: I've not heard this story before. What blessing are you talking about?

Jacob: It was the oddest blessing I've ever heard, not really much of a blessing at all. The stranger gave me a new name: Israel, which means "the one who strives with God." I'm still not sure I understand what happened there. Was it only a dream? Who was I wrestling with all night? A stranger? an angel? God? I named the place Peniel, "the face of God," because that's what I thought I saw.

Esau: I think you are well named by the stranger. You've been striving—struggling and fighting—with God, and with men, all your life.

Jacob: So I have. Most of all, I've been striving with you, my dear brother. I took your birthright and blessing so that I could be first. But the years have humbled me. I now want to live in peace with you and your family.

Esau: Oh, my brother! I have already forgiven you for your thievery and chicanery. If I hadn't, I would have found you and made you pay for it long ago. After you went away to Uncle Laban's, I learned where you were. I overheard it from Mother one day. I could have come to you and killed you to avenge my loss. But something held me back. Perhaps it was the Lord. I think the Lord had something else in mind for us.

Jacob: Esau, your goodness and generosity make me feel small and undeserving. I confess, I was jealous of your closeness with Father. He loved you more because you were a man's man, a hunter of game, while I hated the outdoors. I loved cooking and making clothes, which Father saw as womanly arts.

Esau: And I was jealous of Mother's deep love for you, my brother. Although I hid it well, some of my kindest words to you were spoken through clenched teeth. My thoughts toward you were not righteous.

Jacob: That's all in the past, now! We've both built great fortunes and have sired many children. The Lord has blessed us greatly.

Esau: Even without my rightful blessing from Father, I have accomplished much. Jacob, settle your family near me. I have more than enough land for your cattle and sheep here in Edom.

Jacob: No, my beloved brother. If it were my choice, I would dwell with you until we are both gray with age. But the Lord has come to me in a dream and told me to take my family to a place called Canaan, where our father's father, Abraham, first came. Let us go our separate ways with brotherly love.

Esau: May God bless our families, and through us bless all the families of the earth.

> *O Lord who brings order out of chaos, bring order out of the chaotic events of my life. Open my eyes to your guiding presence in the past. Give me hope for the future. In your name I pray. Amen.*

Questions for Reflection and Discussion

• How would you characterize Esau's and Jacob's relationship as youths? In what ways do you identify with Esau? How do you identify with Jacob?

• How does Jacob's life parallel the nation of Israel's relationship to God? Why is Jacob renamed Israel, "one who strives with God"? In what ways have you struggled with God?

• What brings Jacob and Esau to the point of reconciliation? How are confession and forgiveness intertwined in this story? Who are the people in your life that you need to forgive?

Joseph

Read Genesis 42–45.

SEEING TEN OF MY eleven brothers standing before me after so many years was a shock. It wasn't their appearance that surprised me; they had aged little in my eyes. What stunned me was the sheer power of the emotions that seized me.

I struggled to hide the sudden rage that flushed within me. How could I still be so angry about something that had happened so long before? They had originally planned to murder me. I overheard them plotting while I suffered as their prisoner in a pit. Then, mercifully, they sold me to a passing Egyptian caravan.

Ironically, coming to Egypt as a slave had proved to be my salvation. Had I stayed in Canaan, my brothers would have eventually found a way to silence me. They knew me as Joseph the dreamer. In my youthful arrogance, I freely shared my dreams of self-glorification. I vainly flaunted the colorful coat that Father had given me. I wore it as a badge of Father's favoritism. As one of his two sons by Rachel, I was his favorite and used every opportunity to remind my brothers of this.

My dreams led me to be sold into slavery, and, ultimately, it was my knowledge of dreams that freed me from servitude. An unpleasant incident with Potiphar's wife got me thrown into prison. She tried to seduce me, and when I refused, she accused me of forcing myself upon her. If not for the Lord's guiding hand, Potiphar surely would have killed me.

While in jail, I impressed the Pharaoh's baker and cupbearer with my skills as an interpreter of dreams. Unfortunately, the baker's dream predicted his demise. And the cupbearer forgot about me for two years, until Pharaoh had two dreams that his consultants were unable to interpret.

The Lord's hand must have been guiding these events as well, for the cupbearer spoke highly to Pharaoh of my dream-interpreting ability. When I was told the dreams, their meaning was as clear to me as the sun at high noon. In the first dream, Pharaoh saw seven thin cows and seven fat cows. The thin cows ate the fat cows. In the second dream, Pharaoh saw seven plump ears of corn and seven thin ears. The thin ears ate the plump ears.

None of Pharaoh's wise men or advisers was able to tell him the meaning of these dreams; and yet their meaning was obvious! When summoned to Pharaoh, I told him, "These dreams mean the same thing. They reveal what God is about to do. The seven fat cows and plump ears of corn stand for seven years of abundant harvest. The thin cows and thin ears represent the seven years of famine that will follow."

Seeing that I had Pharaoh's full attention, I continued. "To be prepared for the lean years," I said, "Pharaoh must select a wise man to make sure that one-fifth of the produce from each of the abundant years is stored for the years of famine."

This proposal so pleased Pharaoh that he chose me as the supervisor to carry out this plan. And because everything happened as God gave me the wisdom to predict, I became second to Pharaoh in power and wealth. My power extended beyond the borders of Egypt, since many from other famished countries came to buy grain from Egyptian storehouses.

And that is how I came to see my brothers again. Our father, Jacob, had sent them down to Egypt from Canaan to buy grain for food. After recovering from the trauma of seeing my brothers unexpectedly, I quickly devised a way to repay them for selling me as a slave.

Since they did not recognize me, I questioned them sternly as to where they were from and what their mission was. Then I accused them of being spies. "You have come to scout Egypt, to see our weaknesses!" I said to them. They vehemently denied this charge, but I told them that I didn't believe them.

To prove their truthfulness, they told me more. "We are ten of twelve brothers from Canaan. The youngest is with our father, and the other is no more."

Inwardly, I smiled at their description of me as "no more." Little did they realize, they were now in the power of their "lost" brother. I said to my brothers, "Here is how you can prove that what you are saying is true. One of you go home and bring back your youngest brother, while the rest of you stay here in prison."

I enjoyed seeing them squirm, just as I had writhed in the pit when I didn't know whether I would live or die. After three days, I allowed all but Simeon to go back to Canaan. However, I instructed my servants to fill their bags with grain and to replace the money they had given to buy it. I delighted in the knowledge that this would make them worry about being accused of thievery. I also knew how difficult it would be to convince Father to allow his youngest son, Benjamin, to come back with them. I wanted my brothers to suffer as I had when I rotted in an Egyptian prison for two years.

After many weeks, they returned. I saw from a distance that Benjamin was with them. I released Simeon, who had remained as my prisoner all this time, and he and the other brothers shared a joyous and tearful reunion.

I commanded my servants to prepare a feast. I overheard my brothers anxiously explaining to my steward how they had found their money in their sacks on their journey back to Canaan. I chuckled quietly.

When the feast was ready, I entered the room. My brothers offered me gifts and then bowed low before me. Pointing to Benjamin, I asked, "Is this your youngest brother?" When they nodded, I was so overcome with affection for Benjamin that I fled the room to weep in private. I washed my tear-streaked face, composed myself, and then returned to the feast.

I smirked at my brothers' amazement over being seated in their birth order. Still, they didn't guess who I was. As we made merry at the feast, my heart began warming toward my brothers. I knew then that I would forgive them, but first I would teach them a lesson. Before they left, I instructed my steward to fill each brother's bag with grain and to replace their money. In addition to this, I had my servant put into Benjamin's bag a silver goblet from my table.

After the brothers had traveled a short distance away from Egypt, I sent my steward after them. He accused them of taking a silver cup from my house. Of course, when he searched each man's possessions, he found the goblet in Benjamin's bag. The brothers were in disbelief and agony, for they knew that this would mean Benjamin would be held captive—or worse—and that their father would be heartbroken to lose yet another son.

The steward immediately accompanied them back to my house. When they arrived, I confronted eleven faces contorted with fear and distress. Seeing their agony was almost more than I could endure, but I was determined to carry out my plan. Judah spoke on their behalf. "How can we clear ourselves? We will all work as slaves for you."

I replied, "No, only the one who took the goblet shall be my slave. The rest of you may go home to your father."

Then Judah, my brother who many years before had taken some pity on me and suggested the brothers sell me into slavery rather than take my life, said, "Please, my Lord, be patient with me. You see, we had another brother, whom our father loved greatly. When that brother died, Benjamin, his full brother, became our father's favorite. Only because I gave my word that he would safely return did our father allow him to come with us. If Benjamin doesn't return, our father will die, and we will be the cause of his death. Please, take me in Benjamin's place. I cannot face my father if his beloved youngest son isn't with me."

So moved was I by Judah's words, I could no longer control myself. I ordered my servants to leave and then wept as I had never wept before. The deep pain of years of separation from my father and my brothers was suddenly released in my tears. It was all I could do to say through my sobs, "I am Joseph, the one you sold into slavery in Egypt!"

My brothers' faces showed amazement, disbelief, and fright. I sought to reassure them. "Do not be distressed with yourselves. My coming to Egypt was part of God's plan. Because I prepared for the famine, I am able to save your lives and the life of our father. Hurry and go to our father, and bring him to settle near here in the land of Goshen. There are five more years of famine left, and I want you to be under my protection."

Then I embraced Benjamin, and we wept together. After tearing myself away, I kissed each of my brothers, showing them my love and forgiveness. After the tears subsided, we talked for many hours. I told them the full story of my adventures in Egypt, and they told me news of Father and others from my home country of Canaan.

Never was a reunion so sweet—that is, until I saw Father a few months later. Our eyes met, and we held each other, weeping with joy over the goodness of God.

Almighty God, help me choose reconciliation over revenge. Like Joseph, I have suffered at the hands of others. Yet, as with Joseph, your guiding presence is with me. Inspire me with your love, so that I may love even those who have hurt me. In your holy name I pray. Amen.

Questions for Reflection and Discussion

• As a youth, how did Joseph provoke his brothers' anger and jealousy? Were their actions against him justified? In what ways do you identify with Joseph's anger with his brothers?

• What sufferings does Joseph endure in Egypt? How does Joseph rise to power in Pharaoh's court? When have you used a God-given ability to be successful?

• How and why do Joseph's initial feelings toward his brothers change? What are the "lessons" that Joseph teaches his brothers? What enables you to move from revenge to reconciliation?

II
EXODUS, CONQUEST, AND JUDGES

Moses

Read Deuteronomy 34:1-4.

I AM STANDING ON my final mountain.

For the last time, the Lord has guided my feet up to the heights to address me. This peak is Mount Nebo, high above the plains of Moab. I am standing on Pisgah, an outcropping just below the summit, where I can see across the River Jordan into the Promised Land.

I can see this land the Lord promised to Israel—it is tantalizingly near—but I will never enter it. My mission has been to lead God's people out of Egyptian slavery and into the wilderness where we have wandered for many years, learning the ways of the Lord. My successor, Joshua, will take the Israelites to the next stage of this long journey. He will command them in battle, as they take possession of this land flowing with milk and honey.

This is the second time I have met the Lord on this mountain. I stood here years ago. On that day, the Lord made it known to me that I would not lead the nation of Israel into the Promised Land. I begged to cross the Jordan and set foot on the rich, fertile soil of the land. But the Lord became angry and would not hear of it, because I had disobeyed the Lord at Meribah. I was commanded never to speak of my desire again. But though my lips kept silence, even now my heart cries out to walk in the lovely fields of Canaan.

It was strange to receive such devastating news on a mountain. The holiest moments of my life took place on another mountain: Mount Sinai. There, I met the Lord for the first time in the burning bush that was not consumed with fire. There too I learned the Lord's name. And it was on that mountain that I was called to be the Lord's servant and lead Israel out of Egyptian slavery.

I was terrified of going back to Egypt, where I was wanted for the killing of an Egyptian slave driver. I was frightened to confront Pharaoh, the most powerful ruler in the world. But the Lord would not accept my feeble excuses and sent my brother, Aaron, with me to help with the work of deliverance.

Convincing Pharaoh to let God's people go was nearly impossible, so hardened was his heart. Only after the tenth plague, the death of the Egyptian firstborns, did Pharaoh relent and grant my people their freedom. But after we left, Pharaoh's heart hardened again, and he sent his army after us. In a mighty display of power, the Lord destroyed Pharaoh's army in the Sea of Reeds.

I led the Israelites, kicking and screaming, into the wilderness. One would have thought they would be grateful to escape the shackles of slavery! Yet these malcontents complained constantly. "We're starving," they murmured, and the Lord sent manna and quail to appease their hunger. "We're dying of thirst. Why did we ever leave Egypt?" they grumbled, and the Lord provided water from the rock. I named this place Massah (test) and Meribah (quarrel) because the Israelites tested and quarreled with the Lord. However, I was not innocent at Meribah. I struck the rock too hard with my staff, showing a lack of confidence in the Lord's power.

My highest moment on Mount Sinai came soon after we arrived there. The Lord called to me out of the cloud enshrouding the summit, summoning me to ascend. What happened on the mountain is beyond words; I was in the presence of the Lord and heard the Lord's commandments.

Later, while I was on that same mountain, the Lord gave me tablets of stone containing the sacred words of law. I descended with the stone tablets, only to find that Aaron, bowing to pressure from the people, had fashioned a golden calf for them to worship. I was so angry at this abomination, I hurled the Lord's tablets against the rocks and shattered them! But the Lord's wrath burned even hotter. To punish the wicked, I ground the golden calf into powder, mixed the powder in water, and made the people drink it. Then, as the Lord commanded, I ordered the Levites to kill more than 3,000 Israelites who had refused to obey the Lord. Only my pleading with the Lord saved the Israelite nation from utter annihilation.

One would think that the Israelites would have feared the Lord and learned obedience. But they were so rebellious, we were made to stay forty years in the wilderness. The Lord was so disgusted with the faithlessness of my generation of Israelites that he waited until this generation died before bringing them into the land promised to Abraham, Isaac, and Jacob.

Although we journeyed from Egypt to Sinai, we were not always on the move. We moved from one camp to another, staying for months or even years. We encamped at Sinai for many months. We spent most of our wilderness years at Kadesh-barnea, where there was ample water.

In addition to the law I received from the Lord on Mount Sinai, I received detailed instructions for building the ark of the covenant and the Tabernacle. In the ark, a wooden vessel overlaid with gold, I placed the tablets of law (the Lord had provided another set of tablets after I destroyed the first set). The ark was located in the holy of holies, a part of the Tabernacle where only the high priests could enter. We moved the Tabernacle, a huge tent that functioned as a sanctuary, with us wherever we traveled. It was placed at the center of our camp and surrounded by the priests' tents. The Lord chose to dwell in the Tabernacle from time to time, making it a sacred, holy place.

Being in the Tabernacle was like being on the mountain with the Lord. In the cool darkness of this tent, I loved to spend time in the Lord's presence, praying for guidance and wisdom.

Even though I became the Lord's servant reluctantly, I tried to be a faithful leader of the Israelites. I did my best to judge the many disputes that arose. I instructed the Israelites in the Lord's law. I interceded for them when the Lord's wrath was kindled against them. Having been a shepherd in Midian, I knew the great difficulty of guiding human "sheep." I wasn't perfect (in fact, I made many mistakes), but neither were the people I led. At times, I had to be as stubborn as they were.

Yet through it all, the Lord has been with me. The Lord led me from Egypt to Midian, from Sinai back to Egypt, and back to Sinai again. And now I have followed the Lord's guidance to this final destination, high above the plains of Moab. As I gaze across the Jordan, the walls of Jericho rise in the distance. Beyond Jericho lie the fields of Canaan, where it is said that grain grows as tall as a man. Indeed, this is a land flowing with milk and honey, as the Lord promised. Although I long to set foot on the hallowed soil of the Promised Land, I have accepted the Lord's will. My time of leading the Israelites is now past. I have planted the seeds; others will reap the harvest. And it is a harvest that will not be easily gleaned. The land of Canaan is inhabited by the Canaanites, the Amorites, the Hittites, the Perizzites, the Hivites, and the Jebusites; they will not be pleased by our laying claim to their ancestral land. Joshua and the Israelite army will face a nearly impossible task. But with the Lord's favor, all things are possible.

As I scan the horizon, words of praise come to my lips unbidden. Praise the Lord for his mighty hand in redeeming us from the Egyptians! Praise the Lord for his guiding care in the wilderness! Praise the Lord for the Law that orders our lives! Praise the Lord for his generosity in giving us a land that will sustain us for countless generations! Praise the Lord for the strength we have been given to take possession of the land! I praise the Lord for my life, as prophet, priest, judge, lawgiver, intercessor, shepherd, guide, healer, leader. May I be remembered as one who served the Lord. Praise the Lord!

Almighty and gracious God, show me the Promised Land of your Kingdom. Allow me not only to see it from afar, but to enter it by faith. Like Moses, help me to faithfully serve you all of my days. In your holy name I pray. Amen.

Questions for Reflection and Discussion

• Why isn't Moses able to enter the Promised Land? How do you think he feels gazing across the Jordan and realizing he will not set foot in Canaan? What "Promised Lands" have you seen but not entered?

• In what ways is Moses a great leader of the Israelites? What does he think of the people he leads? When have you been a leader in difficult and challenging circumstances?

• How do mountains play an important role in Moses' life? Reflect on the "mountaintops" of your life. When has God been with you on these mountaintops? How did you feel when you had to come down from these mountains?

Joshua

Read Joshua 6.

I AM RELIEVED THAT this will be our final march around the walls of Jericho. Tramping around this city for the past six days has become drudgery.

Every day we perform the same monotonous routine. The warriors lead the procession; next come the trumpeters; following them are the priests bearing the ark of the covenant; and finally, more guards to protect the rear flank. We march in silence; the only sound is the blaring of trumpets. I'd rather storm the walls now and fight with courage and valor. But the Lord has spoken, and we will follow his command.

Although I trust the Lord's word that the city's walls will collapse, I am anxious about this day, the seventh (and last) day we will march. What if the walls do not fall? If they are still standing after seven days of marching, there will be a rebellion against me as leader of the Israelites. I've overheard much grumbling among the warriors about this strange plan in which we are engaged. Like me, the soldiers are impatient to charge the city and do battle. I have pointed out to my warriors (and to myself) that the walls that stand in our way of conquering Jericho are both thick and high.

I am uneasy also today because Jericho will be the first test of our army in the land of Canaan. Until now, only spies have entered the Promised Land. I was one of the spies sent by Moses (may his name be honored) to scout this land. The other spies complained that the land was filled with giants and could not be taken, but Caleb and I reported that the land would be ours, with the Lord's help. Because of our favorable report, only Caleb and I, of all the Israelites of our generation, were allowed to cross the Jordan.

Moses trained me to take his place after he died, as the Lord had commanded. Moses was our leader for forty years. He lived in the Lord's presence and spoke with the Lord on Mount Horeb (also known as Mount Sinai). Moses gave us the Lord's law and guided the building of the ark and the Tabernacle. Moses was the greatest prophet Israel has ever seen. Yet, it was I who was commissioned by the Lord to lead the Israelites in the conquest of the land the Lord was giving to us; I have sometimes wondered why.

Who can know the mind of the Lord? The Lord's ways are known to us only as he chooses to reveal them. Through Moses, the Lord delivered us from slavery in Egypt. But then we wandered for forty years in the great and terrible wilderness, waiting for an unfaithful generation to die before we took possession of the Land.

Caleb and I alone were still living from all those Israelites who had witnessed the Lord's power parting the waters of the Sea of Reeds when Moses led us out of Egypt. The day we crossed the Jordan was much the same, bright with victory and hope. On this occasion, the Lord used the ark of the covenant to hold back the waters of the Jordan while we crossed.

Following the Lord's command, I selected twelve men, one from each tribe of Israel, to take a stone from the middle of the Jordan. We then set twelve stones at Gilgal as a memorial to remind our nation of the Lord's mighty power in holding back the waters of the Jordan while we crossed.

For a time after crossing, we were overjoyed to be in the Promised Land, a land flowing with milk and honey. Suddenly, we were reminded that the land the Lord had given us was already inhabited by, among other peoples, Amorites, Hittites, Jebusites, and Canaanites. The land was a gift to us, true—but it is a gift that we must now earn in battle. Yes, we must fight for the land promised to our ancestors, Abraham, Isaac, and Jacob. And, if the land is to yield its bounty, we must toil to raise cattle and plant crops.

The Lord's mighty hand has brought us this far, and I trust that he will strengthen our swords as we conquer the land. Why else would the Lord have brought us here?

Even as I reassure myself with these thoughts, I realize that it is time for the final march. On this seventh day, we are to circle the city seven times in silence, except for the blasting of trumpets. Only after the seventh pass will we all be allowed to unleash our voices. At my command, every Israelite will shout with all his might.

On this seventh pass, I notice again the red cord tied to a window on the north wall. This cord marks the home of Rahab, a prostitute, whose family is to be spared the destruction of Jericho. She risked her life hiding our spies during their reconnaissance of the city, months ago. Our spies instructed Rahab to hang the red cord from her window as a sign of protection; this was so that during the siege of the city, our armies would recall Rahab's good deed and save her and her family from destruction. I am reminded of how, years before, Moses had us smear lamb's blood on our doorposts in Egypt as a sign of protection, to escape the wrath of the Lord's final plague against our Egyptian captors.

The seventh pass is ended, and the procession has stopped. All are waiting for a signal from me. The silence seems louder than the blaring of the trumpets. I close my eyes and say a prayer to the Lord for victory in battle. I wonder if the people of Jericho are praying to their god for strength and victory as well.

All eyes are upon me as I raise my sword. The polished broadside of the sword catches the sunlight and gleams. As the sword is poised above my head, I remember Moses raising his staff above the battle with Amalek at Rephidim to inspire the Israelites to victory.

Suddenly, my sword falls as if pulled to earth by a power not my own. I cry out, "Shout! For the Lord has given you this city and all that is in it for destruction!" A mighty roar rises from the people. The priests and warriors are screaming with all their might. The trumpets are blasting an earsplitting fanfare.

The ground begins to shake as the first stone from the walls of Jericho tumbles. Other stones follow until there is an avalanche of rocks. When the dust settles, the wall is in rubble. My voice rises above the din. "Charge!" I shout, and we scramble over the rocks into the city.

So great is the fear of those in Jericho that they offer little resistance. They were relying on the walls for protection. Most of them throw down their swords and flee. But the lust of battle is upon us, and we destroy every one of them, as the Lord commanded; this is to ensure that we remain pure and uncontaminated by the pagan ways of the Canaanites. The priests search each dwelling and collect items made of gold, silver, bronze, or iron for the Lord's treasury.

Remembering the red cord, I summon the two spies who were hidden by Rahab and send them to her house. Rahab and her family come before me, offering tears of gratitude. They will be the only survivors of the destruction of Jericho. Once they are safe, I give my final command. "Set the fires!"

With my warriors I withdraw from the city, and we watch the flames consume it. Even at this distance I can feel the heat on my face from this fiery furnace once known as the city of Jericho. I pronounce a curse upon anyone who tries to rebuild this city destroyed by the Lord's army.

As the flames leap high into the air, I remember the pillar of fire that guided us through the darkness of our wilderness years. Just as the fiery pillar was a sign of the Lord's providence, so the burning of Jericho is a sign of the Lord's victory.

When Moses commissioned me as his successor, he said, "It is the Lord who goes before you; he will not fail you or forsake you." Indeed, these prophetic words have been fulfilled in this first triumph of the conquest of the Promised Land.

Almighty God, give me the courage and valor of Joshua. Strengthen me as I stand against evil in its various forms. May the barriers to doing your will come tumbling down as did the walls of Jericho. In your name I pray. Amen.

Questions for Reflection and Discussion

• What are Joshua's anxieties on the final day of the siege of Jericho? How are those fears overcome? If you were Joshua, what would be your emotions on the seventh day of the march around Jericho?

• What qualities of character does Joshua display as a military commander in the Promised Land? Why do you think he was chosen as Moses' successor? What kind of leader does he become? When have you been called to a place of leadership in the church?

• Why does the Promised Land have to be conquered? What message does the battle of Jericho send to those inhabiting the land of Canaan? Why does modern-day Israel remain the center of conflict and dispute over who has a right to inhabit it?

Naomi and Ruth

Read the book of Ruth.

Naomi

OH, MY BELOVED RUTH. The love that I have for you goes far deeper than that of mother-in-law for a daughter-in-law. You are the daughter I never had.

You have loved me with all your heart and soul. You devoted yourself to me with unshakable resolve. Never in the history of Israel has there been such fierce loyalty and unquestioned fidelity of a kinswoman.

After the untimely death of Mahlon, my son and your husband, my heart ached for you. So did my heart also go out to Orpah, whose husband, and my son, Chilion, also died before his time. You were left alone—without a child to comfort you, and without a brother-in-law who could marry you. I believed that your only choice was to stay in Moab, the land of your birth, and find another husband.

Yet you refused to leave my side. You shared my sadness in the loss of Elimelech, my beloved husband of many years. We were united in a bond of grief, you and I, both knowing the loss of a husband. And putting aside your own grief, you comforted me in my threefold loss of a husband and two sons.

As widows with no sons to care for us, we were truly alone, left to provide for ourselves in any way possible. I finally convinced Orpah to leave my side and make a new life for herself in Moab. But for some reason, you could not do the same. I tried with all my might to send you back to your own people, but you would not go.

I will never forget your words; they echo in my heart:

> Do not press me to leave you
>   or to turn back from following you!
> Where you go, I will go;
>   Where you lodge, I will lodge;
> your people shall be my people,
>   and your God my God.

After hearing these amazing words, I knew we would be together until death took me. Although I said nothing to you, I was overwhelmed by your devotion. I kept thinking, *I am not deserving of such love.* Then, I didn't know that your coming with me to Bethlehem was part of the Lord's design.

When we arrived in Bethlehem the whole town turned out to greet us, two strangers from a foreign land. I announced that I should be called Mara, which means "bitter." My soul had tasted the bitterness of losing the three men in my life. However, another man was about to enter both our lives.

I sensed Boaz's feelings for you long before you did. You thought he was merely being kind because he was my kinsman. You believed that Boaz had his harvesters leave extra grain in the field for you to gather and allowed you to drink from the well on his land simply because of his regard for me. Your heart, so filled with love and kindness, was blind to his longing for you.

I could see that Boaz loved you from the beginning. He loved your devotion to me, and your kindness to all you met. He saw how hard you worked in the fields, toiling without complaint or rest. Yet I also knew he felt he was too old for you.

So I advised you about how to let him know that you returned his affection. I told you to anoint yourself with nard and to put on your best garments. I instructed you to go to the threshing floor and lie down at Boaz's feet after he had fallen asleep after eating and drinking. Trusting me completely, you followed my advice.

I knew that once Boaz realized you returned his love, he would take the necessary steps to marry you as next-of-kin. He had to negotiate with Joash, who was more closely related to me. But Boaz, a clever man, pointed out to Joash that to marry you would dilute the inheritance of his own sons.

My bitterness has now turned to honey! To see you and Boaz so contentedly married makes my heart sing. And my joy is complete because the Lord blessed your union with a son! My line will continue through you, daughter Ruth. I know that your descendants will be renowned.

Ruth

Naomi, my mother. How beautiful is your name to me!

United by tragedy—the death of our husbands—we are sisters in grief. Yet, your anguish is far deeper than mine. To lose a husband is painful enough. But to also lose two sons, as you did, is an agony that I can only imagine.

We took great comfort in each other during our mourning, didn't we? In your goodness, you were more concerned for me than for yourself.

Rather than dwelling on your immeasurable loss, you comforted Orpah and me. You assured us that we would again find love. You lifted our spirits with your humor and shared our tears when we could no longer hold them back.

Why wouldn't I leave you when you begged me to stay among my own people and find a husband? Because the ties that bound us together were more powerful than geography or nationality. I wouldn't leave you because I *couldn't*. So great was my affection, my devotion, my loyalty to you that to leave you would have been like losing my lifeblood.

Deep down, I knew that the Lord, your one God whom I had taken as my own, brought us together for a reason. Although I didn't know what purpose the Lord had in mind for us, I trusted that it would be revealed.

So I journeyed with you to Bethlehem, a place that was only a name to me. Mahlon spoke of it often, remembering the days of his youth. I remember him describing the dire famine that drove all of you to Moab, where grain was plentiful. I remember thinking, *The misfortune of Mahlon's family is my good fortune.* If it were not for the famine, I would never have met Mahlon, or you, Mother Naomi.

Even though I would have traveled anywhere with you, I was glad to return to my dead husband's homeland. Yet I was also afraid of living there as a foreigner. I wondered how a Moabite widow would be received.

I need not have worried. The Lord's hand guided me to glean in a field belonging to Boaz, your husband's relative. He was so kind and generous to me. Even though I was a foreigner, he allowed me to glean close to the harvesters. He ordered the young men to leave me alone, which greatly eased my mind. He allowed me to drink his water, rather than going to a distant well.

Boaz's kindness was overwhelming. When I asked him why he treated a foreigner with such goodwill, he praised me for all that I had done for you, Naomi! I was astonished at this, because I felt it was you who had done so much for me.

Your face came alive with excitement when I returned home that first day. I had more barley than I could carry because Boaz had instructed the young men to pull some handfuls from their bundles for me. You pressed me to tell you how I had come by such bounty. When I mentioned the name of Boaz, your eyes brightened. "He is one of my closest kinsmen!" you exclaimed.

What I didn't tell you (but you knew immediately) was that I was attracted to Boaz. Although he was years older than I, there was wisdom and compassion etched in the creases of his weathered face. But his most desirable quality was gentleness. His kindness to a Moabite woman spoke volumes about his heart.

Even though I didn't speak of my feelings for Boaz, you knew my heart as well as I did. You instructed me in the customs of your people, telling me to lie down on the threshing floor at Boaz's feet after he was asleep. When he awoke, I called on him to perform the obligation of next-of-kin to Mahlon and take me for his wife. To my amazement, Boaz was overjoyed. He said he would gladly do this, but had to negotiate with a kinsman more closely related.

I alternated between elation and anguish over the next few days, worried that Boaz would have to concede next-of-kin rights to this other relative. You assured me of Boaz's cleverness and love for me, calming my troubled heart. Of course, your wisdom prevailed, and Boaz took me for his wife.

Now that our son, Obed, has been born, my joy is perfect. What began in tragedy has ended in bliss. This is all because of the Lord, whom I have come to worship. When I said that your God would be my God, I couldn't know my story would have such a blessed ending.

As I watch Obed lying on your breast, my heart sings with joy. As you have been a mother to me, Naomi, so may you nurture my child with loving care. Who knows what great things he and his lineage will achieve?

Dear Lord, help me learn devotion and loyalty from Ruth's story. Help me appreciate the close ties of family. Teach me to treat strangers with kindness, for this is your will. In your name I pray. Amen.

Questions for Reflection and Discussion

• In what ways can you identify with Naomi's tragic losses? How does she cope with her losses? Why does she want Ruth and Orpah to stay in Moab? What qualities of character does Naomi show?

• What kind of person is Ruth? What binds her so closely to Naomi? What are the positive aspects of Ruth's bond with her mother-in-law? What are the drawbacks? In your life, who are the persons you would follow anywhere?

• What attracts Ruth to Boaz? What attracts Boaz to Ruth? How does Naomi play "matchmaker"? How is Ruth's devotion to Naomi rewarded? Ruth eventually becomes the grandmother of King David— how does this fact affect your understanding of the story of Ruth?

Samson

Read Judges 13–16.

HOUR AFTER ENDLESS HOUR, day after day, I lean against the millstone, pushing in a never-ending circle. I should begrudge the hours of toil, but time means nothing to me. Day and night are merely hollow words. I live in eternal darkness.

After the Philistines captured me, they gouged out my eyes. They thought they were being cruel, but I find blindness merciful. I am not burdened by the distractions of sight. I can't see my captors or the crowds that come to mock and jeer at me. Somehow, blindness lessens my humiliation.

Deprived of my sight I have received insight, something I desperately need. During the endless darkness, I have been thinking, though thinking can be a torment greater than hard labor.

Mainly, I have been thinking about my arrogance and foolishness. Before I was born, my mother dedicated me to the Lord. She raised me to one day embrace the nazirite vows, which she took on my behalf. I was to live as a "consecrated one," set apart by a pure life: no wine, no ritually unclean foods, and no cutting of my hair.

But in my selfish arrogance, I violated each of these vows. I drank wine at the wedding feast of my wife, a beautiful Philistine maiden of Timnah. I ate unclean food: honey from the carcass of a lion I killed with my bare hands. And I foolishly gave Delilah the opportunity to cut my hair, the source of my strength from God.

Why couldn't I have been content to love an Israelite woman? Why was I so drawn to women I was forbidden to love, first my Philistine wife, and then later Delilah? My lustful desires led me down the path of unfaithfulness to my nazirite vows.

I served the Lord by killing Israel's enemies. I slew more than one thousand Philistines with the jawbone of an ass after learning that my wife had been taken from me and given to my best man. The Philistines were no match for the Lord's strength, which coursed through me. But in my conceit, I believed that my strength in battle was my own.

I deserve worse than this fate for telling my secret to Delilah. Would that my eyes had been gouged out before I ever saw her! She was so comely and alluring. Her hair was as soft as a rabbit's fur. Her smile was as bright as the sun at high noon. Because my eyes feasted upon her appearance, I was blind to her wickedness.

For a small fortune, Delilah sold me out to her fellow Philistines. I knew they were seeking a way to capture me. They had tried before and had failed. This time, they succeeded because my desire for Delilah was greater than my resolve to keep my vows to the Lord.

At first I toyed with Delilah, making a game of her craving to know the secret of my strength. I told her to bind me with fresh bow-strings. When the Philistines came to capture me, I burst them as if they were threads. Then, I teased Delilah into tying me with new ropes. I snapped them as if they were twigs. Watching her failures amused me!

But Delilah would not give up. She nagged and begged relentlessly. I almost gave in to her pleas, telling her to weave my hair into seven locks and bind it tightly with a comb. When this failed to drain my strength, Delilah pouted and cried for days. Then she began a new strategy: appealing to my lovestruck heart.

"How can you say you love me and still not tell me the secret of your strength?" Delilah whined. "You have mocked me three times with lies! If you loved me, you would trust me with your secret," she pleaded.

She went on and on about love and trust and how I had humiliated her. Day after day she beat the same drum. I was so infatuated with her, I allowed it. Eventually, she wore me down. I decided to trust her with my secret.

"The secret of my strength is this," I said. "A razor has never come upon my head, because I have been a nazirite from birth. If my head were shaved, I would become as weak as any other man."

As I looked into her eyes, I thought I saw the fires of love burning for me. I realize now that it was greed that inflamed her. Delilah betrayed me as soon as I fell asleep.

But I didn't tell her the whole truth. My strength didn't lie in the length of my hair. Many warriors had hair longer than mine. My strength was in being faithful to the Lord. When I broke my nazirite vow, the Lord's strength deserted me.

How could I, the strongest of men, have been so weak-willed? Why couldn't I, who could kill a lion with my bare hands, summon the power to resist a beautiful woman?

Thinking on this makes my heart as heavy as the millstone I push each day. I am weighed down with sin and guilt. With each step I take, I pray that the Lord will use me to exact revenge against the Philistines, who have taken my sight, my strength, and my honor.

Suddenly, a plan enters my mind as if it were placed there by the Lord. Because I have appeared so weak and docile, the Philistines have allowed my hair to grow back. Each day, I feel a little stronger. This time, I won't betray my secret. I pretend to labor against the millstone.

One advantage of being blind is that the guards speak freely around me, as if I can neither see nor hear. They are talking excitedly of a great feast to their pagan god Dagon on the morrow. Perhaps I will have an opportunity to escape.

The next day, feasting noises from the temple of Dagon drift toward the mill where I am slaving. I feel the sting of a whip. "Samson, you Hebrew swine! The lords have called for you. You are to entertain them!" a guard shouts, laughing scornfully.

I feel hands wrenching me out of the mill, and I am bound with ropes. I am dragged up the steps of the temple like an animal. The guards laugh each time I stumble. "What's wrong, Samson? Can't see too well today?" one of them shouts. I have become a laughingstock.

Finally, there are no more steps. I must be standing in the temple entrance. I hear my name announced, and the crowd cheers. Shouts are hurled from the crowd. "Tell us a Hebrew story, Samson!" yells one. "Dance for us, Hebrew dog!" shouts another. "Show us how strong you are!" another mocks. The crowd roars its approval after each taunt.

I pretend to oblige their requests and offer to dance. I ask a guard to let me place my hands on the pillars for balance. The crowd grows quieter in anticipation of this spectacle. As my hands feel the cool stone of the columns supporting the temple roof, I know what I must do. I pray to the Lord, "Lord God, remember me and strengthen me this last time, so that I can repay the Philistines for my two eyes."

"Dance, Samson, dance!" the crowd chants. I feel a great surge of power coursing through my arms; it is my old strength, returning to me one more time! With all the force I can muster, I push against the pillars. They do not move at first, but I keep straining with all my might. The pillar on my right gives way just a little. This spurs me on to push even harder. The pillar on my right moves. The crowd still jeers and roars with laughter; do they know what is happening? Suddenly, a loud rumbling noise comes from above as the roof shakes.

The Philistines scream with terror as they realize the roof is shaking. Hearing their shrieks inspires me. The pillars are shaking like reeds in the wind! I keep straining against them, intoxicated with the joy of being the Lord's instrument! I hear stones crashing into the panicked crowd. Their cries can barely be heard above the now-deafening noise.

Finally, the pillars buckle, and I know it will be only a moment before I am buried with the Lord's enemies. I am afire with ecstasy! "Let me die with the Philistines," I pray. As I feel the crushing weight of a pillar toppling on me, I collapse in joy. The Lord has delivered me!

Dear Lord, may I learn from Samson a lesson of choices and consequences. May I choose faithfulness to you over gratification of my selfish desires. Help me to serve you in all that I do. In your holy name I pray. Amen.

Questions for Reflection and Discussion

• What kind of person is Samson? How are his personality traits used in the service of the Lord? What leads him to betray his nazirite vows? At what points do you identify with Samson?

• What is Samson's "secret"? What does his uncut hair symbolize? When does he realize that the Lord is the true source of his strength? Why does he recover his strength before he dies? What is the source of your "strength"?

• Why was Samson's story included in the Bible? Why is Samson's story tragic and heroic at the same time? What lessons can be learned from his story? How does the story of Samson speak to you?

Samuel

Read 1 Samuel 1–16:13.

MANY TIMES DURING HER life, my mother, Hannah, told me the miraculous story of my birth. Each time she told it, her eyes glowed with joy and pride. She had endured years of shame for not being able to conceive a child, until she became pregnant with me. Each year, Mother and Elkanah, my father, would go to the sanctuary at Shiloh to offer prayers and sacrifices. There, my mother prayed to the Lord for a child. One year, she not only prayed with her usual passion, she vowed to dedicate her son (if she was granted one) as a nazirite—one whose lifelong vocation would be to serve the Lord. The Lord heard my mother's prayers and granted her the blessing she asked. That is how I came to be.

When I was only a baby, my mother took me to the sanctuary at Shiloh, in accordance with her promise to the Lord, and entrusted me to Eli, the high priest. Thus I was raised in Eli's house. I loved and respected Eli like a father, but his sons were corrupt. Hophni and Phinehas used their authority as priests to steal meat from the offerings of the faithful. They also lay with the women who served in the sanctuary, an act of defilement.

When I was still a boy, I was stirred from my sleep one night by a voice calling my name, "Samuel! Samuel!" I arose and went to Eli's sleeping quarters, and replied, "Here I am!" But Eli said that he didn't summon me and told me to go back and lie down.

Twice more I heard a voice calling my name, "Samuel! Samuel!" and each time, Eli told me the same thing.

The third time, Eli said, "Samuel, it may be the Lord's voice you are hearing. When you hear your name called, reply, 'Speak, Lord, for your servant is listening.'"

Following Eli's instructions I had the most amazing experience. In my mind, I heard the voice of the Lord telling of the doom that would befall Eli's house because of the corruption of his sons. When the voice stopped, I was shaking. I was afraid to tell Eli of my vision, but he insisted that I relate every detail. His face grew grim as I repeated the Lord's words. But Eli only said, "It is the Lord; let him do what seems good to him."

It wasn't long before Eli's sons were both killed on the same day in a battle with the Philistines. When Eli learned of their deaths from a messenger, he fell backward from his seat and broke his neck. I grieved for Eli's loss, but not for his sons.

Because of this vision I had as a youth, I was considered a prophet by the elders of Israel. When I came of age, I was appointed a judge of Israel. To be a "judge" wasn't only to render decisions in legal cases, it was also to lead the people in ways of faithfulness to the Lord. I was not a political ruler, like a king, but more of a religious leader. As a judge of Israel, I banished the Baals and Asherites from Hebrew households and called the people to repent from worshiping foreign gods. I was not always popular, but I was feared and respected because the Lord spoke through me.

In my old age I appointed my sons, Joel and Abijah, to be judges over Israel. I had hoped they would be worthy successors. It was the greatest disappointment of my life that they turned out to be as corrupt as the sons of Eli. I had raised them to be obedient to the law, but they had rebellious hearts. Even though our family was wealthy, they were always hungry for more money, more power, more authority. I tried everything I could to put them on the right path, but without success.

I reasoned that if I put my sons in positions of authority, they would be forced to be responsible. Sadly, I was wrong. They used their power to rob and oppress those they ruled. I hated their corruption, but my love for them crippled me from taking action against them.

Because of Joel's and Abijah's unfaithfulness to the Lord, the elders of Israel begged me to anoint a king. I sought the word of the Lord, and it was revealed to me. The Lord said that Israel's desire for a king was not a rejection of me, but of the Lord. I was instructed to warn the people about the ways of a king, and so I did. I told the people of how kings required many servants and an army to command, and that he would take as he pleased from among them for these purposes. I told them of the taxes that a king would levy upon them. I warned them of how a king would take the best of their herds and flocks for his use.

But the people refused to heed my warning. Again I turned to the Lord. This time the Lord said, "Grant their request and appoint a king over them." So, in the waning years of my life I became a king maker. To find the Lord's choice for king, I was sent to a small town in the land of Zuph. When I arrived there, the Lord instructed me to arrange for a banquet at an inn the next day. I was told that I would see a man from the tribe of Benjamin seeking me at the town shrine.

When I saw a man accompanied by a servant boy walking toward me, the Lord said to me, "This is the one, the man who shall rule over my people." After the man approached me, I told him, "Go up to the shrine before me, and we will eat together. In the morning, I will tell you what is on my mind."

This man, whose name was Saul, looked puzzled. I said, "Don't worry. The donkeys you have been looking for are found. Israel's desire is fixed on you and your ancestral house."

Saul, looking even more confused, said, "I am merely a Benjaminite, the least of Israel's tribes, and my family is among the humblest. Why have you spoken to me like this?"

In silence I took Saul and his servant-boy into the banquet hall and set him at the head of the table. We ate a meal together, enjoying table fellowship. At dawn the next morning, I awakened Saul and we went to the outskirts of the town. Making sure we were alone, I made known the word of the Lord to Saul that he would be king. Saul kneeled as I anointed his head with oil. I then told him the events that would unfold over the next few days, culminating with Saul's being possessed by the spirit of the Lord. After this, I instructed Saul to wait seven days at Gilgal, where I would come and offer sacrifices.

Although it was not something to which I had eagerly looked forward, anointing Israel's first king was a high moment for me. I saw in Saul's youth the hope and promise of our nation. Yet Saul soon proved to be a disappointment. When I was delayed and could not come to Gilgal, Saul took it upon himself to offer sacrifices. He was being pursued by the Philistines, and his army was deserting him. Saul panicked, and in order to keep his army from leaving him, he sought to reassure them that the Lord's favor followed him. I was outraged that Saul had offered this unlawful sacrifice and prophesied that his kingship would not last.

From that moment on, Saul's fortunes faded. He started acting strangely toward others, sometimes showing signs of madness. He exploded with anger at the slightest provocation. However, he was still a mighty warrior in battle.

The final outrage came over the battle with the Amalekites. The Lord commanded me to tell Saul to engage the wicked Amalekites in battle and utterly destroy them and all that they possessed, sparing nothing from the sword. However, when the battle was won, Saul spared the Amalekite king and took the best sheep and cattle. Later, when I questioned Saul about this, he said that he had spared some of the animals to sacrifice to the Lord. But there could be no excuse; Saul had clearly disobeyed the Lord's will. With his act of disobedience, Saul forfeited his crown. When I informed Saul of the Lord's judgment, he repented and begged for mercy. I grieved for Saul and prayed to the Lord with him and on his behalf. But it was too late for Saul's kingship; it was to be finished in just a matter of time.

The Lord instructed me to anoint a son of Jesse the Bethlehemite to be Israel's next king. I filled my horn with oil, took a heifer for sacrifice, and set out for Bethlehem. I invited Jesse and his sons (he had eight) to attend the sacrifice. When I saw the eldest, Eliab, I was certain he would be Israel's next king. He was a mighty man, tall of stature. But the Lord said, "Mortals look on a man's outward appearance, but the Lord looks on the heart."

In turn, each of Jesse's sons passed before me. I did not hear the Lord's voice choosing any of them. Finally, I asked Jesse, "Are all your sons here?" Jesse replied that the youngest was out keeping the family's sheep.

When the youngest son, a handsome boy with bright, shining eyes and a thick mane of hair, was brought before me, the Lord said, "This is the one." Thus, David, a youth, was anointed to be the next king.

Anointing David was my final act as the Lord's prophet and Israel's judge. I went home to Ramah to enjoy my final days. I have had an amazing life serving the Lord. I am grateful that the Lord saw fit to use me, a man of modest talents, to serve him. I have no regrets about dedicating my life to the Lord. There is no better way to live.

Almighty God, grant me the dedication of Samuel. May I hear your voice addressing me in the midst of my life. Give me the resolve to respond to your call by committing myself to you and your way of love. In your name I pray. Amen.

Questions for Reflection and Discussion

• How are the circumstances of Samuel's birth similar to those of the birth of Jesus? Why does Eli recognize that young Samuel is being addressed by the Lord? Samuel's message from the Lord does not hold good news for Eli; when have you been a messenger with words of judgment for someone close to you?

• Why do the Israelites ask for a king? What are the disadvantages and advantages of a ruling monarchy? What causes you to want someone in authority to make decisions for you?

• What kind of king is Saul? Why is Samuel disappointed in Saul's conduct? What is ironic about David being anointed king by Samuel? When has your faith led you to take an action that initially doesn't make sense?

III

MONARCHY

David

Read 2 Samuel 15:1–19:9; Psalm 13:1.

OF ALL THE THINGS I find difficult to endure, *waiting* is the hardest. I am King of Israel and Judah, Sovereign of Jerusalem—the most powerful ruler of my age. Yet even a king must sometimes wait. Should I have led my troops into battle as I did when I was a young warrior? No, I trust my commanders—Ittai, Joab, and his brother Abishai—to carry out my plan. As an old warrior, strategy is now my best weapon.

What am I waiting for? I am awaiting news from the forest of Ephraim, where the future of my monarchy is being decided. In truth, I am waiting for even more urgent news: the fate of my beloved son, Absalom.

I am still stunned that he led this rebellion against me. If he only knew how deeply and how powerfully I love him—perhaps he does know, and doesn't care.

What happened to us, Absalom? We were so close when you were a boy. I was building a kingdom then. Much of the time, I was away from Jerusalem, fighting the Philistines. But the precious hours we spent together were filled with joy and laughter. Did you lose respect for me when I sinned with Bathsheba? I repented of that long ago. The Lord forgave me; why can't you? Are you still angry with me because I refused to punish your stepbrother, Amnon? *Of course* it was wrong for him to rape your sister and my daughter, Tamar. But you have to understand that I *loved* Amnon, my firstborn, as much as I love *you*. I couldn't bring myself to punish him.

Yet you visited revenge on him. I was brokenhearted by the news that one of my sons ordered the murder of another. You bided your time, waiting two long years before avenging Tamar's rape. Can you understand that when Amnon died, part of me died as well? Just as I showed mercy to Amnon, I eventually forgave you and took you back into my house. Do you remember how I greeted you when I summoned you back into my court? I took you into my arms and kissed you with fatherly love.

After our reconciliation, I hoped that you would return my love and affection. I yearned for the closeness that can exist between fathers and sons. But you would not allow me into your life. I would have given you *everything*—could you have been patient. As my eldest living son, my death would naturally mean the beginning of your reign as king. Instead, you resolved to take by force what would eventually have been yours anyway. Why couldn't you wait? Did you despise me so much that to you I was already dead? Or did you assume age had dulled my senses and abilities so that I was weak and slow?

I *was* slow, at first, in catching on to your intentions. When you went to Hebron with two hundred guests from Jerusalem, I didn't realize some would become hostages and others coconspirators. It was clever of you to play on the Israelites' dissatisfaction with my moving the capital of my kingdom from Hebron to Jerusalem; it was for this reason that you set up your base of operations there and organized an army.

I soon learned of my peril and fled Jerusalem. Rather, I staggered out of Jerusalem, stunned that my own son would lead a coup against me. Even in my condition, I had the sense to leave Hushai behind as my spy; and just as Hushai and I had planned, he knowingly gave you unsound advice regarding how to defeat me. Your following his advice to delay before pursuing me gave me much-needed time to assemble my army and plan a counterstrategy. Even more important, I used the time to mend my broken heart over your revolt.

But do you realize how much I still love you and yearn to see you safe? I ordered my commanders to spare you in the battle in the forest of Ephraim so that we may be reconciled to each other. I am longing to embrace you again and bestow my love upon you. I have prayed to the Lord each day and night for your safe return.

And so I pace here between the two gates to the city of Mahanaim, anxious for news of you. With each breath I draw, I say a prayer for your protection. My prayers are suddenly interrupted by the cry of the sentinel, "A man is running toward us!"

I call out, "If he is alone, he is bringing tidings!" (One runner means a message; several runners mean a retreat from battle.)

A few moments later, the sentinel calls out, "There is another man running!" I comment that this also means a message.

Then the sentinel says, "I recognize the running style of the first man. He is Ahimaaz, son of Zadok."

My heart lifts with hope. "I know him. He is a good man and comes with good tidings."

The sentinel is right; Ahimaaz is the runner. As he enters the outer gate and sees me, he cries out, "All is well!" A great weight lifts from my heart. Ahimaaz prostrates himself on the ground and says, "Blessed be the Lord your God, who has delivered up the men who revolted against their king."

Although I am relieved that the battle has been won, there is only one question I need answered: "Is it well with the young man Absalom?"

Ahimaaz replies, "When Joab sent me, I saw a great tumult but couldn't see what was happening." My anxiety returns at this answer. I feel that Ahimaaz is holding something back from me. I tell him to stand beside me and wait for the second runner.

The second runner soon draws near, and I can see that he is a Cushite from Ethiopia. He proclaims, "Good tidings for the king! The Lord has vindicated you this day, delivering you from the power of those who rose up against you."

I ask him the one question that is burning within, "Is it well with the young man Absalom?"

The Cushite answers without hesitation, "May the enemies of my lord the king, and all who seek to do harm to you, suffer the same end met by that young man." The force of his words strikes me as if they were blows from clubs! I stagger to my chamber above the gate, crushed by such grievous tidings.

Once alone, my tears pour out as if from a summer storm. I weep bitterly and deeply. O Absalom, my son! Why couldn't I have died in your place! Your blood is on my hands and your death on my head. If I had been a good father, you would still be alive. If I had spent as much time raising my sons as I did building an empire, there wouldn't have been a need for revolt. If only we had been closer, I could have taught you patience.

I have lost too many sons—Bathsheba's unnamed firstborn, my firstborn Amnon, and now my beloved Absalom. Will the curse that has come upon my house ever end? I am so alone now. My heart is rent by grief that is almost too much to bear. I cry out to the Lord in pain, and my cries echo in the silence.

> How long, O Lord?
>> How long will you hide your face from me?
> How long must I bear pain in my soul,
>> and have sorrow in my heart?
> I have trusted in your steadfast love.
>> Only in you is there salvation and refuge.
> Deliver me, O Lord, from my anguish.

O Lord, comfort me with your presence when I am devastated by tragedy. Enfold me in your love when I am feeling lost and alone. Ease my pain and grief by sharing in them. In your name I pray. Amen.

Questions for Reflection and Discussion

• What makes David's waiting anxiety-filled? What news does David dread more—the loss of his son or the loss of his kingdom? When have you had anxiously to await momentous news?

• What is your explanation for Absalom's rebellion? How did David's actions hurt his relationship with Absalom? What could David have done differently in his family relationships?

• In what ways do you identify with David's grief over the death of his son? How does David's final lament express his trust in God? Where is God in your times of grief?

Bathsheba

Read 2 Samuel 11:1–12:25.

AS I TELL MY story, you must remember one thing: I loved Uriah. Uriah was a good man, a righteous man whose faith was as solid as a cedar of Lebanon. He was deeply honorable and intensely loyal. Ironically, his stubborn loyalty to his fellow soldiers led to his death. But I am getting ahead of myself.

My story begins not with Uriah, but with King David. As a lowly soldier's wife, I had only seen my king from afar. But I was captivated by what I saw. He was many things Uriah wasn't: handsome, well-spoken, and, most of all, powerful. King David's skill both in battle and in affairs of state was legendary. When he was only a youth, he killed the Philistine giant, Goliath. In battle, King David was a courageous warrior, slaying thousands. He was the one who united the northern and southern kingdoms into a single, powerful nation. All of this made him a very enchanting man.

I dreamed that the king would notice me someday. Perhaps he would see me in a crowd as he returned victorious from battle and would inquire as to my identity. Maybe Uriah and I would be invited to a banquet at the palace. These were the silly musings of a young girl. I knew that my desire for King David was sinful, but I could not help myself. In spite of my feelings for the king, I still loved Uriah. King David was the man of my dreams, but Uriah was my husband.

Amazingly, when I met King David, it was not in any of the ways I had imagined. One spring afternoon, I was bathing on the rooftop of our home. I was taking a ritual bath to purify myself after my period. Although my rooftop was in sight of the palace walls, never did I dream that King David was watching me—but he was! Had I known, I would have immediately covered my nakedness. David later told me that he fell in love with me that very moment.

I have been told that I am beautiful, but I never believe such flattery. I am well aware of my flaws, and I have never considered myself a beauty. But who can understand the mystery of attraction? King David thought I was beautiful, and that was enough.

After my bath, there was a knock at my door. Two messengers from the palace arrived with a request that I come and meet the king! I made them wait while, in a frenzy, I brushed my hair, perfumed myself, and put on my finest dress. My heart was racing all the way to the palace.

When I arrived in the king's court, he dismissed his attendants, and we were left alone. As I looked into his eyes, I could see the depth of his desire for me. I was taken aback by the intensity of his gaze. Never had a man looked at me with such raw passion. He said nothing for several moments and then spoke my name. "Bathsheba," he whispered. "What a lovely name for a lovely woman."

I was trembling as he took my hand and led me to his private chambers. I was powerless to resist—not that I wanted to. We made love as if we were trying to consume each other in an inferno of desire. Afterward, I felt horribly guilty about betraying Uriah. I still loved him, but my passion for him compared with David was as an ember to a raging fire. Even so, I tore myself away from David's embrace and fled the palace. So great was my guilt at what I had done, I vowed never to return to the palace.

For weeks, I shut myself in my room, refusing to speak to anyone and eating almost nothing. I wallowed in remorse over my sin and begged the Lord for forgiveness. One day, I was shocked out of this fog of gloom by the realization that I was pregnant! I agonized over what to do and whether to tell King David. Finally, I broke my vow and returned to the palace.

I could tell by the burning in David's eyes that he still desired me as much as before. I told him of my condition, afraid of how he might react: Would he push me away or would he embrace me?

"What are we going to do?" I cried. My fears were calmed as David took me in his arms. He had a plan, as he always did. He would call

Uriah home from the battlefront and make an opportunity for him to visit me. I would make sure that Uriah and I lay together as husband and wife, and then Uriah would believe that the child was his (if he didn't count the months too carefully). I was so relieved!

Unfortunately, this plan failed miserably. When Uriah returned, he refused to sleep with me at home while his fellow soldiers were suffering and dying on the battlefield. Even when King David made Uriah drunk with wine at a banquet, my husband slept among the servants rather than coming home to me. Finally, Uriah was sent back to the battle.

I was devastated at the thought of Uriah's learning of my affair with the king. And he would have known had he not died in battle. My guilt deepened after I learned of Uriah's death; instead of feeling sadness, I felt relief. I observed the specified period of mourning for Uriah, according to Torah.

At the end of the time of mourning, King David again sent for me. Without Uriah, I was free to become one of his wives. As the memory of Uriah faded, my love for David increased. Even though I was pregnant, he ached for me and I for him. We grew happy together.

Then, a dark cloud threatened our happiness. Shortly after our son was born, I learned how Uriah had died. One of my maids overheard the prophet Nathan accuse David of causing Uriah's death. David had sent Uriah into the most dangerous part of the battle with the Ammonites and then had the other soldiers retreat, leaving Uriah to be killed! I fell down as if struck by a blow. The weight of our sin crushed me. If it were not for my union with David, Uriah would have lived! I alternated between loathing myself and hating David.

What my maid didn't have the courage to tell me then (later I learned the truth) were the final words of Nathan's prophecy to David. The punishment for Uriah's murder would be the death of our son! (At the time, all I knew was that our son fell ill.) When David heard of the illness, he went into his chambers and refused to eat. He prayed for our son day and night. On the seventh day of the child's illness, the prophet's words came true: Our baby boy died!

The web of tragedy woven by my adultery, Uriah's death, and my son's death strangled me. I couldn't eat or even speak. I could barely breathe. I was filled with the darkness of grief and remorse. For days, I refused to see David. He stood at my chamber door each day, begging to be let in. Through the door he spoke to me of how grieved he was for what he had done to Uriah. He said that I wasn't responsible for what happened to Uriah, that it was all his fault. He had confessed his sin to the Lord and had been forgiven. He pleaded for my forgiveness. Like a lovesick youth, David proclaimed his love for me.

Even though I wouldn't let him in, I listened to his pleas. He sounded so sincere and so repentant. Slowly, his words began to work their way into my heart, and I realized I still loved him. If God could forgive him, couldn't I do the same? I also reminded myself: With Uriah gone, I had no place to go. And, I had to admit that I enjoyed being a wife of the king, with its accompanying privileges.

So I stayed with David and tried to find it in my heart to forgive him. When David came into my chambers, he spent hours consoling me over the death of our son. On days when I saw only darkness, he brought light and life. He shared some of the prayers he wrote, and I was comforted.

With time and love, I was healed of my grief. Although I would never forget Uriah and the son born of my sin, remembering them was no longer agonizingly painful. One day, I found myself pregnant again. This time, our son did not suffer illness, but was healthy and strong. David named him Solomon, a name that comes from the word *shalom* and means "peace" or "prosperity."

I plan for Solomon to become king after David. Soon, I will make David promise me that, of all his sons, Solomon will rule. David owes me this in exchange for the deaths of Uriah and our firstborn. Already, Absalom and Adonijah are plotting to seize the throne when David becomes old and weak. I vow not to allow this to happen; as I have been a king's wife, so too will I be a king's mother.

O Lord, help me to think through the consequences of decisions before I make them. Open my eyes to the ways my sins have hurt others, you, and myself. Give me the strength to put aside selfish ambition and to do your will in all things. In your holy name, I pray. Amen.

Questions for Reflection and Discussion

• In what ways is Bathsheba responsible for what happened with David? Is Bathsheba a victim or a willing participant in her relationship with David? Do the Scriptures answer this question? When have you acted in a way contrary to your beliefs or values?

• In what ways do the consequences of David's adultery with Bathsheba go far beyond the sin itself? What could David have done differently to avoid having Uriah murdered? When have you made a sin worse by attempting a "cover-up"?

• Once Bathsheba learns of David's responsibility for Uriah's death, why does she remain as his wife? How is Bathsheba able to forgive David for the deaths of Uriah and her son? If you were in her place, what would you have done? What lessons have you learned from Bathsheba's story?

Solomon

Read 1 Kings 1–11.

I AM TOLD THAT I am wise. My reputation for wisdom extends to the farthest reaches of the known world, spreading even to Sheba. My proverbs number three thousand, and I have written more than a thousand songs. I have solved the most complex riddles and have judged cases that would confound a host of sages. I built the great Temple in Jerusalem as well as a palace that shames the Pharaoh's residence in Egypt. I am a master of commerce and trade as well as a brilliant politician.

Yet, for all my wisdom, I am a fool. Here is a riddle: Who is the wisest fool alive? Answer: King Solomon.

I started on the path to wisdom soon after I became the successor of my father, King David. Then I was a naive young man, unable to negotiate my way through the labyrinth of intrigue in my father's court. My mother, Bathsheba, and the prophet Nathan convinced my dying father to name me king rather than my older half brother, Adonijah. Adonijah had already proclaimed himself king, having formed an alliance with Commander Joab and the high priest Abiathar.

As soon as my father pronounced that I was his selection for king, my mother, Nathan, and Zadok the priest rushed me to the spring at Gihon and anointed me with oil. After my anointing, our company paraded back to the city with trumpets blaring and shouts of "Long live King Solomon!" Joab and Adonijah didn't dare challenge my claim at that moment, mainly because I was escorted by my father's royal-palace guard of fierce Cherethites and Pelethites.

Even as a young man, I had enough sense to heed my father's last wishes. He advised me to consolidate my reign by disposing of my ene-mies—including, in particular, Joab, and Shimei, a Benjaminite who had cursed him once. One by one, I had these enemies struck down.

Because I walked in the ways of the Lord, I was rewarded by a vision. In the vision, the Lord offered to grant me whatever I wished. I asked for an understanding mind and the ability to judge between good and evil, so that I might better be able to govern God's people. Because my request pleased the Lord, I was told that I would be given what I asked for and much more. If I kept the Lord's commandments, as my father had, I would also have incomparable riches and honor and long life; so said the Lord.

The Lord kept his promise. I used my God-given wisdom to build a king's fortune. I married foreign wives in order to achieve and strengthen political alliances. Through pacts with Egypt and Tyre, I controlled trade and shipping routes. I developed a lucrative monop-oly on the chariot and horse trade. The result was that my kingdom was rich beyond imagination. A proverb I wrote sums up this early part of my life: "Misfortune pursues sinners, but prosperity rewards the righteous."

Four years after I became king of Israel, Judah, and Jerusalem, I started building the Temple. The Lord had promised my father that his son would build the Lord's house on the site of a shrine that he, King David, had built. The Temple was to be my crowning achievement, a monument to both the glory of God and my father's faithfulness. It took seven years to finish this magnificent edifice of marble and gold, supported by pillars carved from the cedars of Lebanon. More than 100,000 forced laborers were conscripted to do the actual building (including 30,000 Israelites). More than 150,000 stonecutters and laborers worked in the hill country to provide the stone for the Temple.

Once the Temple was finished, the ark of the covenant was placed inside the inner sanctuary. Then the word of the Lord came to me, say-ing, "Concerning this house, if you will walk in my ways, keeping my statutes and obeying my commandments, as did your father, David, then I will dwell with the children of Israel and not forsake them, and I will give you a long life."

Next, I began work on constructing a splendid palace in which to dwell. This palace was to be the jewel of my kingdom. With its Hall of Pillars, Hall of the Throne, and Hall of Justice, the palace dwarfed the Temple in magnificence and magnitude. Rulers came from faraway lands to gaze upon the splendor and glory of Solomon's palace.

Building such massive structures carried a colossal cost in terms of both money and human labor. I was forced to levy heavy taxes on the people of Judah and Israel to pay for the Temple and palace. Still, this was but a small price to pay for forging a world power. Or so I thought then.

At the dedication of the Temple, the Lord graced me with a second vision. After I had given a prayer of dedication, pronounced a blessing on the people, and offered sacrifices of well-being, a great and joyous eight-day festival began. In the midst of the festival the Lord came to me again, as he had at Gibeon. The Lord told me that if I walked with him, as my father David had, with integrity and uprightness of heart, my royal throne would be established over Israel forever. However, if I or my children turned aside from the commandments of the Lord and served other gods, my kingdom would fall into ruins and disaster would reign.

My heart trembled after this vision, because I was not blameless before the Lord. I knew I had been foolish, but I felt powerless to change my ways. The problem was this: I was so enamored with power and the acclaim and comfort it brought, I forgot the Lord. My situation was complicated by my foreign wives. At first, these marriages were political arrangements that cemented Israel's alliances with surrounding nations. I hadn't counted on falling in love with my foreign wives. My devotion to them gave them power over me, which they didn't hesitate to use.

Eventually, I allowed them to worship their various gods: Ra, Baal, Milcom, and Astarte. I gave permission to my wives to build shrines to their gods and to publicly practice their religions. Over time, their devotion to their gods influenced my own faith. Because I loved my wives deeply, I began to attend their rituals. First, I was an observer. What harm could come of watching, I asked? Then, slowly, my heart turned away from the Lord to the gods of my wives.

Their religions were much more colorful and exciting. The Lord was invisible and mysterious, but these gods were earthy and had visible images. The Lord demanded complete obedience, but these gods offered freedom from obedience. Eventually, I became a devotee of Astarte, the goddess of the Sidonians, and Milcom, the god of the Ammonites.

I was a fool, and I knew it. The Lord was patient with me, waiting for me to return to the God of my father, David. But I didn't return. I continued to worship the gods of my wives. My unfaithfulness led to Jeroboam's rebellion, which I barely suppressed. But the Lord told Jeroboam that my kingdom would be torn apart after my death because I had done evil in the Lord's sight.

Because I was foolish, I sowed the seeds of my own destruction. I refused to divorce my foreign wives and reject their gods. To do so would have been political suicide for my kingdom. Instead of being concerned about the kingdom of the Lord, I was obsessed with the kingdom of Solomon.

The end of my days is in sight, for I am growing weak and weary of this world. My legacy has been established: I will be remembered for my wise sayings and discerning judgment. Even more, I will be remembered as the builder of the great Temple in Jerusalem. But in my heart, I know that I have not followed the Lord's ways in all things. And whoever does not follow the Lord's commandments is truly foolish. I face death knowing that I am Solomon the fool.

Almighty God, give me a wise and discerning heart as you gave Solomon. Strengthen my determination to be faithful to you. Help me see that genuine wisdom is following your ways and turning away from other gods. In your name I pray. Amen.

Questions for Reflection and Discussion

• What does Solomon mean by saying that he is a wise fool? In what ways does Solomon demonstrate wisdom? How is he foolish? How would you define *wisdom* as it is used in this chapter?

• Compare and contrast yourself with Solomon. What characteristics do you share with Solomon? How are you different? In what ways would you like to be more like Solomon? In what ways do you want to be less like him?

• How does Solomon sow the seeds of the division of the unified kingdom? What should he have done differently? How does God use Solomon's desire for riches and glory to accomplish God's purposes? How does God use your selfish desires for good purposes?

Jezebel

Read 1 Kings 16–21; 2 Kings 9:30-37.

I HATE THEM! I DESPISE them! I abhor them! These foreigners. These—Israelite *dogs!* But of all of them, *Elijah* is the one I detest the most. Thank Baal he is dead. Unfortunately, he didn't die before doing unspeakable evil to my husband and me.

Elijah is the reason I am sitting in this tower in my dead son's palace in Jezreel, waiting for Jehu. Jehu served in the army of my husband, King Ahab. Yesterday, Jehu killed my son, Joram, in Naboth's vineyard. And so I wait for Jehu to find out whether I too will die.

Everything would have been different if it weren't for Elijah. It was he who tormented my husband, Ahab, with predictions of drought and defeat in battle. It was he who caused the murder of the four hundred prophets of my god, Baal. And, it was Elijah who prophesied my husband's death.

Why did I ever come to this godforsaken place? I, the princess of Phoenicia, the daughter of Ethbaal, King of the Sidonians and high priest of Astarte! My marriage to Ahab was political, arranged by Ahab's father, Omri, and my father. Both Israel and Phoenicia were threatened by the growing power of Ben-hadad, King of Aram. The alliance my marriage to Ahab formed protected our nations, but *I* was the one who had to pay.

Ahab was tolerant of my worship of Baal. He didn't ask me to give up my religion and to adopt the worship of his God. He even allowed me to erect altars to Baal and to import my own priests. I loved Ahab for indulging me. Perhaps he really did love me as well.

As I started to win converts to the worship of Baal among the Israelites, Elijah appeared. What a terrible sight he was, dirty and ragged, with a long, matted beard! He wore strange clothing made of camel hair, and you could smell him coming long before he arrived. When I first saw Elijah, I thought he was simply crazy and harmless. That was my fatal mistake.

Elijah was a man possessed with great evil power. When he spoke, it was as if he was in a trance; his eyes rolled back in his head as he spat out his words. My husband called him "Troubler of Israel" and "My Enemy." I called him "My Tormentor."

It would have delighted me to have killed Elijah. After my four hundred prophets were slaughtered at Elijah's command, I was so enraged that I put him under a death sentence. Alas, he fled into the desert and hid like the scared rat that he was.

It was the taking of Naboth's vineyard that proved to be the downfall of my husband, Ahab, and the end of my reign as queen of Israel. Naboth was a simple old fool who owned a lovely vineyard next to the palace. For years, Ahab had coveted this lush land, bursting with the fruit of the vine. So one day I said to him, "Ahab, go and speak with Naboth. Perhaps he will sell you the land if you offer a fair price."

The next day, Ahab arose early, as eager as a child, and went to Naboth's house. I expected Ahab to return with the deed to Naboth's property in hand, task successfully accomplished, as he was accustomed. So I went about my usual routine, not giving the matter another thought.

Later that day, I was walking down the corridor beside the king's bedroom and saw Ahab lying face-down on his bed. His head was turned away from the doorway, and I thought I heard weeping. The servant who was stationed at the door said to me in a frightened whisper, "The king refuses to eat."

I sat down on the bed next to my husband and asked, "Dear Ahab, what makes you so sad that you will not eat?"

Without turning to face me, Ahab said, "I spoke to Naboth this morning. I said that I would either buy his vineyard for money or I would give him another vineyard in trade. But he said that he would not give up the land!"

"Why?" I asked, genuinely puzzled.

"In our land, a man is forbidden by law to sell or trade his ancestral inheritance," Ahab whined.

"I've never heard of such an idiotic law! Aren't *you* the king of Israel? And don't *you* decide which laws are to be obeyed and which are not? Get up and eat. I will get you Naboth's vineyard." Ahab arose, wiped his face, and smiled. He might not have been so pleased had he known of my plan.

That very hour I wrote letters under Ahab's name to the elders and nobles of Jezreel. The letter proclaimed a fast, which signaled that a grave crisis was upon us. Also in this letter, I instructed the elders and nobles to assemble, to seat Naboth at their head, and to find two scoundrels to falsely accuse Naboth of cursing God and the king. Issuing these orders under the king's authority and seal ensured that they would be carried out. When I sealed the letters with Ahab's seal, I sealed Naboth's death sentence. According to the Israelite law, the penalty for cursing God was death by stoning.

Within a week, my orders were carried out to the letter. Naboth was dead, and the vineyard was ours. When I received word of Naboth's death, I told my husband, "Go and take possession of your vineyard. Naboth no longer has need of it." Ahab rode out of the palace like the wind, delighted with his new possession. But a short time later, he returned not as a triumphant warrior, but as a beaten man.

"What is wrong *now?*" I asked when I saw his slumping shoulders and agonizingly slow walk.

"Elijah. Elijah saw me at Naboth's and knew what we had done. He called me a murderer and pronounced God's judgment upon *both of us!* He said that my house would be like that of Jeroboam, that death and destruction would come upon us. And—he said that *dogs* would lick up our blood after we were killed!"

Then, Ahab would speak no more. He tore off his royal robes and put on sackcloth, walking around the palace as though he were already dead. Nothing I said or did could break this death-spell of Elijah's. And when Ahab led his forces into battle against the nation of Aram a short time later, Ahab was killed by a bizarre shot from an enemy archer.

And now I wait for Jehu, who no doubt will be my executioner. But if I must die, I will die proud and unbowed, and with hatred of Elijah burning in my heart! He is to blame for the desolation that has come upon Ahab's house. I will not die as a cowering child, but as a proud and victorious queen! Earlier, I had my maidservant paint my eyes and adorn my hair with flowers. Jehu is calling for me outside my window. I must go.

Almighty God, forgive me when I give my allegiance to gods other than you. Like Jezebel, I have cared more for power than for people, more for prestige than for righteousness. Cleanse me so that I might do your will. In your holy name I pray. Amen.

Questions for Reflection and Discussion

• Why is Jezebel so furious with Elijah? Is her anger justified? In what ways can you identify with Jezebel's anger at Elijah? When has anger caused you to take drastic actions?

• What is Jezebel's role in stealing Naboth's vineyard? Why does Ahab allow her to carry out her evil plan? Where do you see the abuse of power in our society?

• How does Jezebel prepare to face death? Which of the following words would you use to describe Jezebel: *defiant, desperate, dignified,* or *devious?* If you have time to prepare, how will you face death?

IV
WISDOM

Esther

Read the book of Esther.

I WAS SECRETLY THRILLED when Mordecai told me I must go to the citadel with all the other young virgins of Susa. But I didn't convey my excitement to Mordecai, who seemed worried. "You must not tell them you are a Jew," he warned.

I trusted Mordecai and would obey him in this. He was actually my cousin, but he had been like a father to me ever since my parents died. I was so young when they died, I don't even remember their faces. I couldn't imagine having a better father than Mordecai. In a way, he was also like a mother, worrying over every detail of my life.

Although everyone else called me Esther, my Persian name, Mordecai called me Hadassah, my Hebrew name. He taught me the Torah and raised me to worship the one God. Since we were living in a foreign land, we were not open about our religion. We feared persecution by those who didn't understand. Mordecai told me the story of how our great-grandfather, Kish, had been carried away from Jerusalem by the army of Nebuchadnezzar, the powerful Babylonian king. When Cyrus, the Persian king, conquered Babylon, my people began living under Persian rule. Now, King Ahasuerus reigned over Persia.

The reason I was so excited about going to the citadel was that King Ahasuerus was seeking a new queen. I heard rumors at the market that the queen would be chosen from the virgins gathered there. Who wouldn't want to be queen of a great empire?

When I arrived at the citadel, it seemed that every young woman in

Susa was there. My heart was pounding as we were lined up. The king's eunuch, Hegai, walked down the line looking at us carefully. When he came to me, he paused and inspected me intensely. Then he said to a guard, "Take this one to the palace."

I couldn't believe I'd been chosen! I soon learned that I would be a part of the king's harem. I also discovered that none of us would set eyes on the king for one year. In that year, we would be groomed by beauticians and trained in the ways of royalty.

Although I was honored to be chosen for the king, I deeply missed Mordecai. One of the eunuchs told me that Mordecai waited each day at the entrance to the palace hoping to hear how I was faring. Through different eunuchs, I sent him reassuring messages.

On the day I was taken before the king, I was petrified. However, Hegai's training helped me appear to be composed and poised. And the beauty treatments must have worked; when the king set his eyes upon me, he seemed very pleased with my appearance. I couldn't have dreamed how much I would please the king. A few days later, he set the royal crown upon my head and made me his queen! He even held a great banquet in my honor for all of his important officials.

A few days after I became queen, I received an urgent message from Mordecai. He had overheard two of the court eunuchs plotting to murder King Ahasuerus! I immediately told the king what Mordecai had discovered, and an investigation took place. The two would-be betrayers were hanged. I was relieved that the king was safe, for I had grown fond of him.

I was happy beyond imagining. Every day, I woke up wondering, "Is this a dream?" I couldn't believe that I was *Queen* Esther. As queen, I was attended by a court of maids who catered to my every need. I wore lush royal robes and planned official banquets. I was living every young woman's dream.

But my dream was soon threatened by a nightmare named Haman. Haman was a minor official who had politicked his way to the top of the king's court. Soon after I became queen, he was promoted to the position of First Official. Haman was obsessed with power and demanded that everyone—except the king, of course—bow down when he passed.

Shortly after Haman was promoted, I heard that Mordecai, who still spent his days at the king's gate waiting for news of me, refused to bow down to Haman. Worshiping anyone other than Yahweh was forbidden by the Torah, the Jewish law handed down from Moses, which Mordecai obeyed with all his heart. I feared for him. Unaware, I should have feared for myself as well.

One day, one of my maids came to me with the news that Mordecai was at the king's gate, clothed in sackcloth and ashes. He was weeping and lamenting with loud and bitter cries. This news upset me greatly, and I sent my eunuch, Hathach, to find out what was troubling Mordecai.

When Hathach returned with the reason for Mordecai's distress, I was stunned. Haman had convinced the king to approve a wicked plan to destroy all Jews living in Persia. Apparently, Haman had paid a huge sum into the king's treasury in exchange for a decree allowing all Jews to be killed on the thirteenth day of Adar, the twelfth month of the Jewish year! Could the king have approved such a plan with full knowledge of it? I could scarcely believe what I was hearing.

Hathach told me another thing also that sent a chill down my spine: Mordecai wanted me to approach the king to put a stop to this decree. He was asking me to risk my life! The penalty for approaching the king without being summoned is death. Only if the king then holds out his golden scepter will the unsummoned person live.

I sent Hathach to Mordecai with this news, and he returned with a chilling response from my adoptive father: "Do not think you will be safer in the king's palace than any other Jew. If you keep silence, many Jews will perish, but we will ultimately be delivered. Who knows? Perhaps you have become queen for just such a time as this."

I pondered these powerful words and decided to take the risk. Three days later, I put on my royal robes and went into the king's inner chamber. This was it: I had broken the king's inviolable law; would I now be condemned to die? When King Ahasuerus saw me standing in the court, he held out his scepter. My knees almost buckled with relief! So happy was the king to see me that he said, "What is it that you desire, Queen Esther? I will grant your request even if it is half of my kingdom."

I replied, "If I have won the king's favor, please come tomorrow with Haman to a banquet I have prepared. There I will make my request." The trap was now laid; I could only hope Haman would step into it!

Later that day, I heard the sounds of hammering and sawing. Through my window, I saw a gallows being built in front of Haman's house. When I inquired of my maids the reason for this, they told me that Haman had built the gallows to hang Mordecai because of his refusal to bow down to Haman.

At the banquet, after the king and Haman had eaten an excellent meal and enjoyed fine wines, the king asked me, "What is your petition, Queen Esther?"

I chose my words carefully. "If it pleases the king," I said, "let my life be given to me, and the lives of my people. We have been sold, I and my people, to be killed and annihilated."

The king was incredulous and asked, "Who has presumed to do such a horrible thing?"

I said, "He is sitting here. It is Haman who has done this!"

Suddenly, the king jumped up from his couch and in a rage stormed off into the garden. Then, Haman threw himself on the couch where I was reclining and took hold of my feet, begging for mercy. The king returned from the garden and saw Haman struggling with me. "Do you dare assault the queen in my house?" the king cried out to Haman.

Harbona, one of the king's eunuchs who knew me well, said, "Look, the very gallows that Haman prepared for Mordecai, who saved the king's life, stands outside."

The king said, "Hang Haman on that."

The next day, Mordecai and I approached the king, who immediately held out his scepter. I politely reminded the king that his decree against the Jews was still in force. Amazingly, the king said to us, "I will give Queen Esther all that Haman possessed. Mordecai, you will take Haman's place in my court. Your first act will be to write as you please regarding my edict concerning the Jews. You may seal it with my ring, and thus it will become law."

Mordecai wrote a decree that allowed the Jews to defend themselves against their enemies on the thirteenth day of Adar, the day Haman had chosen for our destruction. When that day came, the Jews triumphed over their enemies, for the Lord was on our side. The next day was a day of great joy, gladness, and thanksgiving. A feast was proclaimed for Jews to celebrate throughout the ages, to remember the day that was turned from sorrow to gladness, and from mourning into a celebration. We called it Purim (because Haman had cast *Pur*—that is, a lot—to decide the day on which we would be destroyed).

Mordecai was right: I *had* become queen for just such a time as this.

Dear Lord, give me the strength and courage of Esther, who risked her life for her people. When my resolve to do what is right falters, steady my spirit. Help me to grasp those moments when I am called to act at "such a time as this." Amen.

Questions for Reflection and Discussion

• How is Esther's path to royalty like a fairy tale? When have you experienced unexpected good fortune? What emotions did you have in reaction to this good fortune?

• What kind of person is Haman? Who have been the "Hamans" in your life? Have you been the victim of prejudice because of your race or religious beliefs? If so, when?

• What does Mordecai mean by "perhaps you have become queen for just such a time as this"? How does Esther show inner strength and courage? In what situations have you needed the strength and courage of Esther?

Job

Read the book of Job.

WHY, LORD, WHY?
I cry out in agony and hear the echo of my own words.
I beg for answers, but there is only silence.
My God, have you forsaken me?
If you are hiding from me, please come out into the open,
So I can find comfort in your majesty and solace in your wisdom.

Everything I love has been destroyed.
Everything I care about has perished.
My beloved sons and daughters are gone, crushed by a mighty wind.
Who sent the wind?
My sheep and servants have been consumed by fire.
Who sent the fire?
And now, I am covered with oozing sores.
Who sent this affliction?
Lord, I'm not accusing you of the violence that has come upon me.
I'm not charging you with crimes against humanity.
You are the Creator of all that is good and the Provider of justice.
I'm not holding you accountable for sending these torments upon
    me.
But who *is* responsible for these monstrous travesties?
And *why* were they visited on me?
You know me, Lord, better than I know myself.
You know that I am a righteous man.

You know that I worship you with all my heart, mind, soul, and strength.
You know that I love my neighbor as I love myself.
You know that my heart is kind and good.
So—why?

It has taken all my strength to resist my wife's advice.
"Curse God, and die," she said.
Yet, still, I cannot blame you for the evil that has been visited upon
    me.
I am struggling to accept what has happened as a mere accident, a ran-
    dom event.
But how can so much misfortune occur in one life?
And don't you rule the chaos, bringing order from it?

My so-called friends have provided explanations for my suffering.
They are certain I have done something to bring these calamities upon
    myself.
They are so certain that you reward the righteous and punish evil-
    doers;
they would not be so confident of their assumptions if they were in my
    place.
Eliphaz says, "You had it coming to you, Job."
He is certain that you are punishing me for my sins.
He advises me to search my heart to see where I have gone wrong.
"You *must* have sinned," he says.
When I maintain my innocence, he accuses me of undermining our
    faith.

You know, Lord, that I'm innocent of the evil Eliphaz assumes of me.
I am not perfect, but I have never done anything so wrong as to
    deserve this.
My suffering is without end.
I am allotted months of emptiness and nights of misery.
I loathe my life!

"God punishes the wicked," Bildad lectures.
Bildad begs me to repent of my sins.
God is just, he says. If I will repent, God will restore me.
Repent of *what*, I want to know.

O Lord, if I could just put you on the witness stand, you would clear
my name.
You would vouch for my loyalty and dedication to you.
If only I had an advocate to argue my case, I know I would win.
I know that my redeemer lives, somewhere.
Yet I am left alone to defend myself.

"Wickedness always receives just retribution," Zophar claims.
I point out that many of the wicked thrive and prosper!
They gain their wealth by lying and cheating.
They care nothing for widows and orphans.
They live longer than many of the righteous.
If the wicked are always punished, would that I receive their punish-
ment of prosperity and length of years!

I am telling my friends the truth!
They are unwilling to admit even the possibility that good is not
always rewarded and evil is not always punished.

If only I could return to the days of my youth, before these tragedies
came upon me.
We were close then, Lord, you and I.
Now we seem so far apart.
Who has moved away—you or me?

I curse the day of my birth!
If only I had known the road ahead, I would never have set out on the
journey.
I am the most accursed of men, a laughingstock and a mockery of
righteousness.
I will spend the rest of my days suffering on this ash heap, awaiting the
sweet embrace of death.

Why won't you speak to me, Lord?!?
I can't take this silent treatment much longer.
If you would address me, then I could understand your counsels and
find answers in your wisdom.

Suddenly, a whirlwind swirls near.
A voice speaks, and I am addressed.
The voice asks me questions I cannot answer.
The voice puts me in my place.
I can only be silent before the awesome power of the Lord.
The voice pauses, and I admit my own inadequacy.
Then, the questioning continues.
In my silence, I realize that the Lord's wisdom is more magnificent
    than I can comprehend.
God is God, and I am merely a mortal;
the finite cannot grasp the infinite.

I hear myself apologizing to the Lord.
I did not know, I confess, how wonderful you are.
I did not realize how great is your wisdom.
I did not understand your awesomeness.
I beg your forgiveness for questioning your silence and doubting your
    justice.

My fortune has now been restored twofold.
I have a new family now—not that they can replace the loved ones I
    have lost to death, but there is hope in new life.
And I have been made whole.
I could not have endured the Lord's silence much longer.
Now, I know who I am and how fragile and precious life is.
Most of all, I know that the Lord did not abandon me in my distress.

*Dear Lord, help me to remain faithful to you when I suffer. When
tragedies happen, help me to turn to you for comfort rather than blame
you for what has happened. May I be as honest as Job in my prayers.
In your holy name I pray. Amen.*

Questions for Reflection and Discussion

• What questions does Job ask of God? How can such questions be
answered? When have you questioned God? What kinds of "answers"
did you receive?

• How does Job express his anguish? What roles do his friends play in Job's suffering? When you are suffering, how can friends help ease or increase your pain?

• What range of emotions does Job experience during his suffering and restoration? How does God address Job's afflictions? When have you experienced God's grace in painful and difficult circumstances?

Koheleth

Read the book of Ecclesiastes.

Vanity of vanities! All is vanity and a chasing after wind. Everything is wearisome. What has been is what will be. There is nothing new under the sun.

Our lives are but a breath, quickly carried away by the wind. Everyone will eventually be forgotten. Only God endures. Only God's wisdom is eternal.

I AM CALLED KOHELETH, the Teacher. Some have found wisdom in my musings. Others say I am an old fool. But I care nothing for the judgment of mortals, whether favorable or not; only God's approval matters.

From the days of my youth, I sought to learn the secret of contentment. My search has taken me to many different places, both geographically and spiritually.

When I was a young man, I was certain I would find contentment through wealth. I worked hard and accumulated a small fortune, which grew into a large one. Soon, I possessed riches beyond measure. I built grand houses and planted fertile vineyards. I delighted in the wines made from my vines. I created gardens the size of a small forest, with sparkling streams and glistening pools. Each night I was entertained by singers whose songs were enchanting. The pleasures of the flesh were as near as the snap of my fingers. I indulged my every desire. I wanted for nothing.

I enjoyed every known indulgence. And still, I was not satisfied. I was bored and restless with my life. It was then that I began my quest for Wisdom. I was desperate to find the key to its many-roomed mansion. I pursued it as a suitor would pursue his beloved.

At first, I traveled the world and experienced every new thing I could, hoping Wisdom would reveal itself to me. I spoke with kings and princes. I conversed with those deemed wise and with those derided as fools. I read the sacred scriptures of the great religions, scouring them for genuine Truth. Yet, chasing Wisdom was as futile as chasing the wind.

Soon, I became a keen observer of life. I became a student of the world and learned many truths. I learned that the wise and the foolish die the same death and are soon forgotten. I discovered that there is a time and place for every matter under heaven. I saw that it is better to be dead than to be oppressed. I observed the unfairness of life—how the righteous suffer while the wicked prosper.

I composed a poem of my observations:

> The race is not to the swift,
> nor the battle to the strong,
> nor bread to the wise,
> nor riches to the intelligent,
> nor favor to the skillful;
> but time and chance happen to them all.
> For no one can anticipate the time of disaster.

In my travels, I discovered much wisdom, but the greater Wisdom eluded me. I found many truths, but not *the* Truth.

After years of pursuing Wisdom in the world, I returned home. This time, I didn't indulge myself in luxurious pleasures. Rather, I lived plainly and simply. Instead of seeking Wisdom outside, I looked deep inside myself to see if it could be found there.

I withdrew from the world and became a solitary individual. Except for my servants, I rarely saw another person. I spent day after day meditating on my life. I became immersed in my inner life. I took long walks in my gardens, oblivious to the beauty surrounding me because my eyes looked only inward. Yet, in my solitariness, Wisdom eluded me. Then, I realized that being alone is *also* vanity and chasing after wind. Solitary people are no better off than those surrounded by family and friends.

I began to comprehend the value of friendship. Two are better than one in many of life's pursuits. Work is more engaging with two. With two, there can be mutual support and help in a crisis. Two can withstand a calamity or an attack better than one. So I renewed my friendships and found my life enriched. Yet, I still didn't have the key to unlock Wisdom's door.

In frustration, I gave up my search for Wisdom. I had sought Wisdom every place I could think of, both within and without. I had dedicated many years to finding its secrets. But Wisdom's Truth still escaped me.

Amazingly, once I abandoned my search, the Truth about Wisdom came to me. While enjoying a meal with a friend, I stopped chewing in mid-bite. An awesome serenity came over me. It was as if a fog had lifted from my vision and I could see clearly for the first time in my life. What came to me in that moment was this: Wisdom is a gift of God. Wisdom cannot be earned or achieved. Human wisdom is severely limited. Only in God is there true Wisdom and genuine Truth.

Suddenly, I understood that what I had observed about life is true, but not the whole Truth. All *is* vanity and a chasing after wind. Life *is* filled with ambiguities and contradictions. Life *is* overflowing with unfairness and injustice. There *is* no simple explanation for all that happens, good or evil.

Therefore, the only wise response to the vanity of life is this: *Eat, drink, and find enjoyment in your toil.* That is, be satisfied with what God has given you, whether much or little. Riches cannot bring happiness. Pleasures cannot fulfill you. Self-indulgence is not the way to contentment. You cannot change the injustices and tragedies that befall you. Be satisfied with the small blessings of daily living. Be grateful for your daily bread. Appreciate the taste, texture, and aroma of a good meal. Cherish the fruit of the vine that lightens your heart. Value the satisfaction that comes from a good day's work. Treasure the companionship of friends.

I understand now that small truths can add up to *the* Truth. Although human wisdom is inadequate to discover God's Wisdom, it's the best we've got.

As word of my musings on Wisdom spread, young men who were seeking to hear what I had learned began coming to me. At first I sent them away. But as more came, I took pity on them and allowed the most earnest of them to stay. These young men were so much like I was: restless, anxious, yearning for a contented life. They would sit at my feet for hours while I spoke to them about the vanity of life and the joys of eating, drinking, and working. This is how I received my name, the Teacher.

I am very old now, and the years weigh heavily upon me. I know that my life will soon become a breath, carried away by the wind. But I am content in the shadow of death. For I know that both life and death are gifts of God, the Source of all Wisdom.

Dear Lord, help me to receive your gift of Wisdom and to embrace your Truth. Save me from vainly seeking contentment through wealth, pleasure, or power. Give me the strength to follow your way of new life. I pray this in your name. Amen.

Questions for Reflection and Discussion

• Why does Koheleth proclaim that "all is vanity"? Where does he search for contentment? Why does he find contentment to be elusive? Where have you searched for contentment?

• What leads to Koheleth's quest for Wisdom? How does he go about seeking Wisdom and Truth? What insight does he gain about Wisdom? How have you sought Wisdom in your life?

• What is the Truth about life that Koheleth discovers? How does this Truth set him free? When has the Truth freed you to live fully and joyfully?

V
PROPHETS

Elijah

Read 1 Kings 17–19.

I AM WANDERING DEEPER, deeper into the wilderness. The sun is becoming hotter by the hour, and I have no water to quench my growing thirst. I'm a day's journey from Beersheba, where I left my servant. I feel lost and alone—so utterly alone.

I have come to the wilderness to die. My ancestor, Moses, led our people into the wilderness, and many died here, including him. I want to join my ancestors, for I am no better than they were. As I sit down in the shade of a broom tree, I voice my desire as a prayer: "Please let me die, Lord."

Lack of food and water has left me exhausted. I drift into a fitful sleep and dream of Queen Jezebel standing over me with a sword. I see a flash as it arcs toward my neck, and—suddenly I'm awake, drenched with the sweat of fear.

I have fled to this desolate place to hide from Jezebel, Queen of Israel and worshiper of Baal. She has sworn to avenge the deaths of the four hundred and fifty prophets of Baal I had put to the sword.

Just one day ago, I faced the prophets of Baal in a contest to prove whose god was truly God. Would the Lord or Baal prevail?

I had the prophets of Baal prepare a bull for sacrifice on an altar of wood, and I did the same with another bull. We were to use no fire to ignite the wood. The prophets of Baal would pray to their god, and I would pray to the Lord; and whoever answered the prayers with fire would be declared the true God.

The prophets of Baal prayed fervently all morning long, begging their god to answer them. When Baal was silent, they screamed and cut themselves with swords until their blood ran freely. When Baal still didn't answer, I commented, "Perhaps your god is meditating, or on a journey, or he is asleep and must be awakened." Noon arrived, and no fire came from Baal, a god who exists only in its prophets' imagination.

Then it was my turn. I built an altar using twelve stones, representing the twelve tribes of Israel. Next, a trench was dug around the altar. Then wood was placed on the altar, with the bull on top. To prevent any accusations of trickery, I had my assistants drench the bull and wood with water, three times, until the water trickled down to fill the trench.

At the appropriate moment, I prayed to the Lord, the God of Abraham, Isaac, and Israel. The fire of the Lord fell on the altar and consumed everything—the bull, the wood, even the stones and water in the trench! The people of Israel fell on their faces and exclaimed, "Indeed, the Lord is God."

I saw the prophets of Baal flee. "Seize them, and don't allow them to escape!" I yelled. When they were captured, I had them brought down to the Wadi Kishon and ordered them executed by the sword.

When Queen Jezebel, the wicked wife of King Ahab, heard about this, she was enraged. She vowed, "May the gods do to me what Elijah did to the prophets of Baal if I do not make his life like theirs by tomorrow!"

And so, I fled for my life. How could a prophet who had been the instrument of a great victory for the Lord flee from a mere mortal? I have no answer. All I know is that I was terrified of Jezebel and fled into the desert like a mongrel dog.

Because of the heat and my exhaustion and weakness, I fall asleep again. When I awaken, I find a warm cake and a jar of cool water next to me. I devour both and fall into a deeper sleep. When I awake again, a voice tells me, "Get up and eat. You must have strength for the journey ahead."

I am led by the Lord to Mount Horeb, a long journey that takes forty days and forty nights. Once there, I come to a cave to await word from the Lord. The next day, the word of the Lord comes to me as a question: "What are you doing here, Elijah?"

I answer, "I have been zealous for you, Lord. But the Israelites have forsaken your covenant, thrown down your altars, and killed your prophets. I alone am left, and they are seeking to kill me."

The voice commands me, "Go out and stand on the mountain, for the Lord is about to pass by."

I wait on the mountain for the Lord. Suddenly, there is a violent wind so strong that trees are uprooted and rocks are split apart; but the Lord is not in the wind. Then, there is an earthquake that shakes the foundations of the mountain; but the Lord is not in the earthquake. Next comes a blazing fire that consumes trees and grass; but the Lord is not in the fire.

After these tumults, there is sheer silence. I strain my ears to listen. I hear a voice as soft as the whisper of a gentle breeze. The voice asks, "What are you doing here, Elijah?"

I answer as before: I am the only faithful one left in all of Israel, and I have come here to die before I am killed by Jezebel.

The voice speaks again. I have to be absolutely quiet to hear it. "Go, and return on your way to the wilderness of Damascus. There, you shall anoint Hazael as king over Aram. Next, you shall anoint Jehu as king over Israel. Then, you shall anoint Elisha as your successor. Finally, you should know that there are seven thousand knees in Israel that have not bowed to Baal."

After hearing this, I no longer want to die. I feel a newfound courage welling up within me. The Lord has restored my purpose for living. My feet are light as I leave Mount Horeb. Strengthened by the Lord's presence, I resolve to face Ahab and Jezebel. No longer do Jezebel's threats frighten me. I will pronounce the Lord's words of judgment upon her and Ahab. I am leaving one wilderness for another.

Some time later, when my business is finished in Damascus and I prepare to leave for Samaria, I receive word that Ahab and Jezebel have violated the Lord's laws once again. It seems that Ahab desired the vineyard of Naboth because it was next to his palace. Naboth refused to sell because the law forbids selling one's ancestral inheritance. When Ahab complained to Jezebel, she bribed witnesses to testify against Naboth at a trial. They lied: "He cursed God and the king." Naboth was taken out of the city and stoned to death.

Walking on the road to Jezreel, where I will meet Ahab, the word of the Lord comes to me again. I am to say to Ahab, "Have you killed, and also taken possession? Thus says the Lord: 'In the place where dogs licked up the blood of Naboth, dogs will also lick up your blood.'" Concerning Jezebel, the Lord's word is this: "The dogs shall eat Jezebel within the bounds of Jezreel."

My legs feel heavier as I approach the road to Naboth's vineyard. Even though I will speak the truth to Ahab, it is difficult to deliver such news. I take no pleasure in pronouncing Ahab's demise. However, a prophet of the Lord cannot choose what to say or not to say. As the Lord's instrument, a prophet must play whatever melody the Lord provides. Sometimes I play the harsh tones of judgment; other times, the welcome notes of forgiveness.

My time is drawing to a close. My successor, Elisha, has been appointed. I will use the time I have left to teach him the ways of a prophet of the Lord. Only the Lord knows what lies in store for him— and for me.

Almighty God, who was with Elijah in the wilderness, sustain me during my wilderness times. Strengthen me with your presence. Grant me the courage to speak truthfully and live truly. In your name I pray. Amen.

Questions for Reflection and Discussion

• Why is Elijah so afraid of Jezebel's threat after winning the contest with the prophets of Baal? In what ways is he in a "spiritual" wilderness? When have you been in a spiritual wilderness?

• In what ways does the Lord sustain Elijah? What is the significance of Elijah's encounter with the Lord outside the cave? Where do you most often seek God's presence—in mighty acts of power or in "sheer silence"?

• While in the wilderness, what mission does Elijah receive from the Lord? How is Elijah different after emerging from the wilderness? What parallels are there between Elijah's and Jesus' wilderness experiences (see Matt. 4:1-11)? How has the Lord sustained you in your wilderness times?

Isaiah

Read Isaiah 6:1-8.

In the year that king Uzziah died, I saw the Lord sitting on a throne, high and lofty.

WHAT IS THIS VISION of light that fills my mind? It comes so unexpectedly, without warning. I was in the Temple for my daily prayers. As I approached the altar, I saw the Lord sitting high above it on a throne. The Lord's robe filled the Temple, and there were six-winged seraphs—celestial beings—flying around above the Lord.

It was all so—overwhelming. I fell down on my knees in awe and wonder.

And one called to another and said:
"Holy, holy, holy is the LORD of hosts;
the whole earth is full of his glory."

When the seraphs spoke, their voices shook the foundations of the Temple, and the entire sanctuary was filled with smoke. Suddenly, I was overcome with a sense of my own sinfulness. I felt filthy kneeling before the pure presence of the Holy One of Israel, the Lord. My guilt was too much for me to bear, and I cried out,

"Woe is me! I am lost, for I am a man of unclean lips, and I live among a people of unclean lips."

In that moment, I knew with painful certainty that I was a sinner whose only hope was the mercy of God. I had hurt others, willfully and knowingly. I had not been generous with my possessions. I had tolerated the evil that flourished around me: the poor not earning enough wages to buy food to eat, the widows and orphans being forgotten, the rich thinking only of adding to their fortunes. But, most of all, I knew that I had offended the Holy Lord who demands purity and righteousness from every person.

> Then one of the seraphs flew to me, holding a live coal that had been taken from the altar with a pair of tongs. The seraph touched my mouth with it and said: "Now that this has touched your lips, your guilt has departed and your sin is blotted out."

At first the fire from the coal felt icy, as frigid as a winter's night. After that, the burning began. This was a purifying flame, as when a rotting stump is burnt. It was as if my guilt was consumed by the fire and I was free! Then the heat spread from my lips across my entire face, and I felt as if I were afire; and I *was* aflame, with the Spirit of the Lord's presence. Then there was a burning in my heart, a fiery desire to do the Lord's will and work. Not only were my sins consumed by this inner heat, my will was ablaze to do whatever the Lord commanded.

> Then I heard the voice of the Lord saying, "Whom shall I send, and who will go for us?" And I said, "Here am I; send me!"

The Lord's voice sounded thunderous, yet it wasn't deafening. It was the voice of wisdom and power, the voice of glory and might. And I heard something else, too, in the voice of the Lord: love. Yes, there was deep compassion woven into the mighty voice of the sovereign God. What else could I say to the Lord but "Send me!"

Many years have passed since I received the Lord's call in the Temple. Accepting God's call turned my life onto a new road. I became the Lord's prophet, speaking words of judgment and words of hope to God's people. When I saw the evils around me, I deplored them in the Lord's name. When I saw King Ahaz attempt to save our nation by making an alliance with Assyria, I condemned his unwillingness to rely on the Lord's protection. After Ahaz ignored my advice, I spoke no prophetic words for twenty years. When Ahaz died and his son Hezekiah took the throne, I emerged from my silence to warn him away from the mistakes of his father. For three years I went naked and barefoot as a sign of what would happen to Egypt and Ethiopia, who had created an alliance.

It has not been easy being God's mouthpiece, especially when I must chastise my own people for their sins. But from the beginning of my call to serve as the Lord's prophet, I knew that we are an unclean people in desperate need of the Lord's purifying fire.

However, the Lord did not only speak words of judgment through me. I proclaimed words of hope as well. I saw a day when all nations and peoples would flock to the mountain of the Lord's house and beat their swords into plowshares. I proclaimed that a remnant of Israel would survive the coming destruction and establish a new kingdom of trust in the Lord. I prophesied that a coming leader, the Messiah, would bring endless peace to our world by showing us the ways of the Lord.

All of that which I proclaimed for the Lord could be contained in these words: *Trust in the Lord, for only in the Lord is salvation.* No wonder I was named Isaiah, which means "the Lord is salvation."

Almighty God, help me hear your call and respond with the answer, "Send me." Touch my spirit with a fiery desire to do your will and work. Send me to the people and places that need to hear your word of judgment and grace. I pray this in your holy name. Amen.

Questions for Reflection and Discussion

• If you were in Isaiah's place, what would your reaction be to the vision he received? Terror? awe? wonder? joy? confusion? When have you been startled by encountering the Lord's presence?

• What are Isaiah's first words to the Lord? When have you felt "lost" and "unclean"? What takes your sin and guilt away?

• What happens when Isaiah's lips are touched with a burning coal? What is Isaiah's response to being forgiven? When have you proclaimed, "Here I am; send me"?

Jeremiah

Read the book of Jeremiah.

I DIDN'T SET OUT to speak words of doom and destruction to the people of Israel and Judah. If I had had a choice, I would have prophesied peace and prosperity. Rather than proclaim the wrathful judgment of God, I would have preferred to speak gentle words of reassurance.

Given the choice, I think, no one would become a prophet of the Lord. As the Lord's prophet, I have been treated as a pariah. It would have been better for me to have leprosy than be a prophet; at least lepers receive a measure of sympathy. Because of the harshness of my prophecies I have been imprisoned and, at one point, sentenced to death. The kings of Judah, their ears burning from my words, tried to get rid of me several times, but the Lord would not allow it.

I have resigned myself to living a life apart from my people. The Lord instructed me to refrain from marrying and having children. My only true friend over the years has been Baruch, who recorded the words the Lord spoke through me. Baruch has been more than a scribe to me; he has been a source of strength and comfort. He is my rock. I know that even if the nation I love persecutes me, Baruch will stand by my side.

As I said before, no one would *choose* to be a prophet. This was especially true for me. The Lord called me to be a prophet when I was but a youth. When I objected that I was only a boy, the Lord said,

"Do not say, 'I am only a boy';
for you shall go to all to whom I send you,
and you shall speak whatever I command you."

Then the Lord touched my mouth and said,

"Now I have put my words in your mouth.
See, today I appoint you over nations and over kingdoms,
to pluck up and to pull down,
to destroy and to overthrow,
to build and to plant."

Unfortunately, I did more destroying and overthrowing than I did building and planting. I was only speaking the words the Lord put in my mouth. Could I help it that they were mostly words of condemnation and denunciation?

Although I was never able to convince my people of this, it was *their* sin and disobedience that caused me to prophesy such severe rebukes. Israel and Judah were rampant with corruption. Like adulterous prostitutes, they were unfaithful to the Lord's covenant. They worshiped the idols and false gods of foreign peoples. They neglected the widows and orphans in their midst and oppressed the poor. Never were a people so deserving of God's judgment.

When I first became the Lord's prophet, I saw signs of hope. King Josiah was a devout man and followed the Lord's ways. After finding a lost scroll of the Torah, he launched a great religious reform in Judah. There was a renewal of trust in the Lord and obedience to the Lord's law. But Josiah, fighting to reestablish the kingdom of David, was slain in a battle at Megiddo.

Josiah's reforms, so promising at the beginning, were rejected by the sinful people he ruled. Like blood draining from a wounded king, the lifeblood of Josiah's reform seeped away after his death.

Why are God's people so blind? Can't they see that repentance is their only hope? If they would forsake their evil ways, and turn again to the Lord in total obedience, the Lord would not destroy them. The Lord is merciful to those who obey him, but will judge with impunity those who forsake his ways. The Lord is our Potter, and we are clay in his hands. The Lord has formed us, shaping us into a chosen people. Yet, we have become a broken vessel, shattered by our disloyalty and wickedness.

After Josiah died, the Lord told me that war would soon come upon Judah. Disaster after disaster would befall this disobedient people, until they were subjugated to Babylonia. But the people of Judah refused to hear the Lord's words and paid dearly for their deafness.

At the coronation of Josiah's older son, Jehoiakim, I preached against putting our faith in the Temple for deliverance. The Judahites felt that the Lord's Temple would save them from destruction. But I knew the truth: The Lord saved only those who obeyed him. My sermon so incited the priests and prophets of the Temple that they demanded my execution. At my trial, I repeated my sermon and warned my accusers of the dire consequences if I were put to death. Fortunately, the princes and the people rallied on my behalf, and I was spared.

When I prophesied that Judah and Israel would be conquered by Babylonia, I reached the lowest point of my popularity. When Carchemish fell to the Babylonian King Nebuchadnezzar, I knew that the fate of Judah was sealed. Since I had been banned from the Temple, I asked Baruch to read the scroll of my indictment of Judah. King Jehoiakim was so upset that he cut the scroll into pieces and fed it to the fire.

After I learned of this incident, I rushed to the Temple in Jerusalem and spoke an oracle of doom on the city. Pashhur, the high priest, was so angered that he had me beaten and put in stocks. The next day, I delivered a scathing indictment of Pashhur and was released.

In time, that which the Lord had revealed to me through prophecy came true. King Jehoiakim had refused to pay tribute to Babylonia and later died under uncertain circumstances. (Some say he was assassinated.) Jehoiakim was succeeded by his young son, Jehoiachin. But within three months' time, King Nebuchadnezzar's Babylonian armies had laid siege to Jerusalem. Jehoiachin was captured and taken to Babylon as a captive, along with most of the royal family and other leaders. Jehoiachin's uncle, Zedekiah, became king; but Zedekiah had been chosen by and was under the control of the Babylonian King Nebuchadnezzar. It was only a matter of time before the Lord's word was fulfilled.

During the siege of Jerusalem, the Lord had instructed me to put on a yoke and proclaim an oracle of doom on the city. The yoke symbolized the Lord's instruction to us to submit to the authority of Babylon. However, the prophet Hananiah publicly challenged me by giving false assurances of the imminent and speedy defeat of Babylon. When

I disputed Hananiah, he took the yoke from my shoulders and broke it. Later, after receiving new instruction from the Lord, I returned with a yoke of iron bars and condemned Hananiah's false assurances. Later that same year, he was struck down by the Lord and died, just as I had prophesied.

A few months later, Nebuchadnezzar's army had captured the surrounding towns and renewed the siege of Jerusalem. Speaking for the Lord, I advised everyone to submit to Babylon, to cooperate and be taken by Nebuchadnezzar's armies into exile in order to save their lives. Because of my words, the princes called for my execution. I was cast into the bottom of a muddy cistern, but I was rescued a few days later.

The walls of Jerusalem were breached a few weeks after this. Many, including Zedekiah, were taken as exiles to Babylon. Because I counseled surrender to Babylon, I was released to travel freely in Judah. I went to live in nearby Mizpah, where I spoke the Lord's word again. The Lord told me to proclaim, to the small group of Judahites still left: "Remain in the land and throw yourself on the mercy of the Babylonians."

This prophecy enraged the princes, who took Baruch and me captive. They called us traitors to our heritage and took us to Egypt against our will. There, I continued to speak the Lord's word of judgment on all nations. No nation would escape the Lord's wrath. Though Babylon had prevailed for now, the day of its defeat was coming. Egypt would not be spared; neither would Moab or Philistia. All were under the Lord's judgment.

Now, at the end of my life, the Lord has put into my mouth the words of hope I so desperately longed to speak. I have prophesied the return of the exiles and the restoration of Israel and Judah. Jerusalem will be restored to its former glory and its walls rebuilt. Even though they rebelled against the Lord, the Lord has not forgotten or forsaken his people.

Sadly, there are few left to hear my prophecies of the restoration of Israel. Baruch, of course, has recorded them to be read to God's people in exile. So perhaps I will gain, after I am departed from this life, what I could not have while here: the approval and affection of my own people. However, the approval of others is a small thing when compared with the Lord's favor. I pray that I have spoken truly the Lord's words during my life. For what finally matters in this life is obeying the Lord in all things.

Dear Lord, grant me a measure of Jeremiah's courage. Help me to speak the truth, even when I become unpopular as a result. Remind me that your words of judgment are spoken in love, so that your people return to you. I pray this in your name. Amen.

Questions for Reflection and Discussion

• Why was Jeremiah so exasperated with his people? What were their primary sins? What was the goal of Jeremiah's prophecies against Israel and Judah? To what degree was this goal achieved?

• In what ways do you identify with Jeremiah? What emotions does his story evoke in you? If you were Jeremiah, how would you feel about your mission and ministry?

• What trials does Jeremiah face as a result of his prophetic message? What enables him to endure and prevail over these difficulties? When have you faced difficulties because of speaking the truth? How did you endure these challenges?

Daniel

Read the book of Daniel.

AS I REMEMBER THE years of my life, I am in awe of God's power and love. I have been the most fortunate of God's servants. I have served four kings of the great empire of Babylon, and yet I never bowed down to worship these kings or their gods. I serve the One, true God, the God of Israel, whose steadfast love has given me strength and courage.

A large measure of both strength and courage was required to endure the trials that came to me as an exile from Judah. My lone regret is that I was forced to live out my years in Babylon. As a young man, I was seized from my father's home in Judah and taken east to Babylon. This was done at King Nebuchadnezzar's command because he wanted some young Israelites to train for service in his court.

Fortunately for me, my three dearest friends—Hananiah, Mishael, and Azariah—were taken with me into exile. They were given Chaldean names: Shadrach, Meshach, and Abednego. My Chaldean name was Belteshazzar. The Chaldeans took away our names, but they could not take away our faith in God.

Our first trial came immediately after we began our three-year training program in Nebuchadnezzar's palace. The first day, we were given the food and wine rationed to all trainees. I refused to eat this food because it violated the dietary laws of our faith. I raised this issue with the palace master, a compassionate man who reluctantly refused to change our diet. He was worried that our appearance would suffer and that we would look less healthy than the other trainees. Eventually, I was able to convince the guard in charge of us to allow us to eat vegetables and drink water for ten days, and to then compare our appearance with the appearance of the others. At the end of the ten days, the four of us looked healthier than the other trainees, and so we were allowed to continue our diet.

After three years, Shadrach, Meshach, Abednego, and I were brought before King Nebuchadnezzar. Noting how strong and healthy we were and hearing the wise words that God had given us, the king granted us positions in his court. We were delighted to serve in the most magnificent palace in the world, with its hanging gardens and bubbling fountains. However, we soon discovered that serving a pagan king was a dangerous challenge.

Nebuchadnezzar was plagued by dreams that disturbed his sleep. He commanded the wisest sages in his court to describe his dream (without having been told of it!) and then interpret it. When none could do this, the king became so enraged that he sentenced all of the city's wise men to death. My friends and I were ordered to help carry out the execution.

Horrified, I questioned Arioch, the executioner, about what had happened. I immediately requested an audience with the king to interpret the dream. That night, my companions and I prayed to God in heaven that the dream and its interpretation be revealed to us. The next day, praise God, I was able to describe the dream and its interpretation. The sages were spared their lives, and my three friends and I were promoted to the highest positions in the king's court.

Unfortunately, this intensified the Chaldean officials' envy of us, mere foreigners who had risen above them. When Nebuchadnezzar made a giant, golden statue and commanded that everyone worship it, I knew we were in trouble. Immediately, the jealous officials ran to the king and told him that Shadrach, Meshach, and Abednego refused to bow down to the idol. The king was enraged. My friends were bound and thrown into a furnace that had been stoked to seven times its normal heat. The guards who cast them into the furnace perished from the heat. But miraculously, Shadrach, Meshach, and Abednego emerged from the fire with not a single hair singed; God had been with them! Nebuchadnezzar was so impressed, he decreed that no blasphemy against our God would be tolerated.

After Nebuchadnezzar died, his son Belshazzar sat on the throne. He was a pompous and arrogant ruler who loved to host grand banquets. At one such banquet for a thousand lords and the king's wives and concubines, Belshazzar served wine from the gold and silver goblets ransacked from the Jerusalem Temple before it was destroyed. The revelers praised the gods of silver and gold, further defiling God's vessels of worship.

Immediately after this abomination, the fingers of a human hand appeared and wrote four words on the wall: *MENE, MENE, TEKEL,* and *PARSIN.* I was summoned to interpret the writing. I knew the writing was from God, and I trusted God to reveal to me the proper interpretation. The first word, *MENE,* meant that God would quickly bring an end to Belshazzar's kingdom. *TEKEL* meant that the king had been found lacking in character. *PARSIN* meant that Babylon would be ruled by the Medes and Persians. That very night, Belshazzar was killed, and Darius succeeded him.

Darius the Mede was a wise and good king. However, some of the same officials who had sent my three friends to the furnace plotted to have me killed. They convinced Darius to issue an ordinance and enforce an interdict condemning to death anyone who, for the next thirty days' time, prayed to a god or a human other than the king.

Although I knew of this order, I continued to pray to God in my house three times a day, as I always had. The conspirators discovered me praying and dragged me before the king. Darius was grief-stricken that I had been trapped by his decree; and by Median law, the king's command, once sealed, could not be revoked. King Darius spent the entire day with his advisers seeking a way to save me. Finding no way around the law, I was sentenced to be thrown into the lions' den. Before the door shut behind me, the king cried, "May your God, whom you faithfully serve, deliver you!"

I was frightened by the lions. All night, they would come near and sniff me. As I knelt and prayed, I could feel their hot breath on my neck. Yet my God shut their mouths, and I was spared a horrible death.

The next morning, King Darius, who had spent a restless night, anxiously cried out to me through the door, "Daniel, has your God delivered you from the lions?"

I could hear the hope and fear in his voice. I replied, "O king, may you live forever! My God sent an angel to shut the mouths of the lions, and I am not harmed."

Darius was elated, and he was so furious with those who had

entrapped me that he threw them—along with their wives and children—to the ravenous lions, who immediately devoured them. Darius also issued a decree that all people in his kingdom should be in fear and trembling before God.

It had been during the first year of Belshazzar's reign that I began to receive visions from God. The first vision, of four giant beasts rising up from the sea, terrified me. Directly, the fourth beast was destroyed by an Ancient One, and the power of the other three beasts was taken away. I was told by an angel that the four beasts represent four kingdoms. The Ancient One represents God's kingdom that will endure forever. Even though the kingdom of God triumphed in my vision, I still trembled with fear.

Another vision came to me a few years later. This time, a giant ram was destroyed by a goat. The goat sprouted four horns, representing four kings. From one of the horns a small horn sprouted, representing a blasphemous king who refused to allow burnt offerings in the Temple. This sacrilegious king was to be destroyed by hands not human. For days after seeing this vision, I lay sick. When I finally recovered, I was dismayed because I didn't understand the vision.

I received more visions during the time of my service to Darius and Cyrus. Some of these visions symbolized and interpreted present events; other visions made predictions about the end. These visions are too long to tell here, but I have written them on a scroll to be preserved for the ages.

While I am honored that God entrusted these mysterious visions to me, I am also afraid of them. Persecutions of God's faithful will come before God establishes an everlasting Kingdom. My advice to those who would serve God is to stand steadfast against all that is evil and to serve God only. If we are faithful to God, then we will be given the strength and the courage not only to endure, but to triumph. Amen and amen.

O God of power and might, give me the power to endure difficult times. Grant me the character of Daniel, who was courageous and loyal in times of trial. When my hope fades and my spirit is troubled, lift me up with your steadfast love. In your name I pray. Amen.

Questions for Reflection and Discussion

• What qualities of character does Daniel demonstrate during his years in exile? How does he make the best of a difficult situation (being in exile)? In what ways does Daniel's faith in God help him thrive in a foreign land?

• What are the challenges Daniel and his friends face because of their faith in God? How is their faith put to the test? When has your faith been tested, and how did you cope?

• What are the themes of Daniel's visions? What similarities do you see between Daniel's visions and the vision of John in the New Testament book of Revelation? Why are such visions both frightening and reassuring at the same time?

Amos

Read Amos 1–5; 7:14-17.

I AM TORMENTED BY tears of sadness and tears of rage. Why won't the people listen to me? Day after day, I stand in the square at the center of Bethel and shout until I am hoarse and exhausted. I tell them of the gathering storm of God's wrath. I warn them of the terrible consequences of their refusal to repent and return to the Lord. They hear, but they do not listen. They look, but they do not see.

They remind me of the sheep I used to care for.

Yes, I was a shepherd of Tekoa when the Lord called me to be a prophet. Before that, I was a dresser of sycamore trees. I was not raised to be a prophet. Nor did I belong to one of the guilds where prophets were trained to hear and to speak God's word to the people. I am a prophet only because God wanted it to be so.

But how painful it is to speak God's word day after long day and not see that word obeyed. The Israelites believe that they will escape the Lord's judgment because they are God's chosen people. What they do not realize is that they were chosen for *obedience* to God!

Have they not seen what happened to the other nations that refused to repent? Are they blind to the lessons of the Edomites, the Ammonites, the Moabites, and, especially, the people of Damascus? The fire of the Lord consumed these disobedient nations. With Assyria as the sword of the Lord's judgment, they fell like slain soldiers in battle. Why do the Israelites now think that they will escape the same fate?

Some believe that they are immune to God's judgment because they

126

are rich. They believe that their wealth is a sign of the Lord's favor and that riches will protect them. How foolish and blind they are!

They trample the poor into the dust as they ride in their chariots.
They shove the sick and infirm out of the way as they go to pray
   in the Temple.
They buy and sell the needy like fruit at the market.
They profane God's altar with stolen garments and wine bought
   with the spoils of dishonesty.

The only thing I can do is warn them: "The day of the Lord is coming!" They expect this day to be a great day of vindication and celebration; they couldn't be more wrong. This will be a day of God's judgment on sin. On that day, the fire of the Lord's judgment will burn and purify, as in the refining of silver! On that day, the roar of the Lord's wrath will consume those who are wicked! On that day, the arrow of God's Word will pierce the armor of self-justification! On that day, *there will be no excuses!* The light of the Lord's truth will shine as brightly as the blazing sun at noon.

I am infuriated with my own people. My heart burns with the wrath of the Lord. The people have forsaken the ways of the Lord, pretending that God will not notice. They have forgotten the Torah and the righteousness it demands. They prefer injustice to justice simply because it suits their whims.

They *must* return to the Lord and live; but these are people who prefer death to life! They *think* that they are alive, but they are wrong! True Life is obedience to the Lord and doing justice by one's neighbor. True Life is sharing one's bread with the poor and showing compassion to the widow and the orphan. True Life is living as God's child.

Would that God's people return to the Lord and live; my heart breaks for them. Like sheep, they have wandered away from the Lord and are ignorant of the terrible dangers that lurk in the shadows. They do not see the power of their enemies. They are blind to their moral decay. Like a sycamore fruit that is rotten on the inside, they are deceived by the external signs of health and wealth.

I long for the day when God's people understand the seriousness of their sins and repent. Do they not know how offensive their disobedience is to the Lord? Have they not heard that God is a God of righteousness? Do they think that they will escape the fate of the Edomites and Moabites simply because they themselves were born in Israel?

They believe that they can atone for their sins by simply bringing fruits and animals to the altar and observing the festivals. They put on sackcloth and cover themselves with ashes. They show all of the external signs of repentance, but they are not sincere. The Lord looks upon the *heart!* Our God *despises* falseness. The Lord *hates* hypocrisy! A thousand insincere burnt offerings cannot equal one handful of grain given in genuine remorse over sin. Why won't they listen to me? Why won't they believe the Word of the Lord? Why do they rush headlong to destruction without thinking?

And so I weep tears of sadness and tears of rage for God's people. Perhaps someday they will return to the Lord. Perhaps someday they will wake up from their sleep and see how deeply they have offended the Lord. Possibly then, they could be raised from the living death in which they dwell.

I will continue to speak the word of the Lord, even though it falls on deaf ears. I will take my place in the square and prophesy until my voice is worn out with fatigue. I will try to lead these sheep out of the wilderness of sin and into the pastures of obedience to the Lord.

With my dying breath, I will speak the Lord's word!

Almighty God, help me to hear your word in whatever form it comes to me. Give me the strength to obey your word, even when I am commanded to do what is difficult and painful. Like Amos, help me to be faithful even when I am rejected and despised by others. In your holy name I pray. Amen.

Questions for Reflection and Discussion

• What different emotions does Amos experience as the Lord's prophet? When have you felt righteous anger at injustice or disobedience?

• Why don't the Israelites heed the Lord's warnings given through Amos? When have you felt immune from criticism and judgment? What broke through your "shell of immunity" and caused you to see the truth?

• In his prophecy, Amos speaks of sheep as similar to people. How are people like or unlike sheep? What does it mean for us to pray, "The Lord is my shepherd" (see Psalm 23)?

Jonah

Read the book of Jonah.

WHEN THE LORD COMMANDED me to warn the Ninevites of their impending doom, I was dumbfounded. Why would the Lord bother with these unclean foreigners? They deserve to be wiped off the face of the earth as soon as enough brimstone can be gathered!

The unsavory reputation of the Ninevites (who are pagan *Assyrians*) is common knowledge. They are guilty of the abomination of idol worship, believing that images made of stone and wood have supernatural power. Their gods have strange names like Shamash, Sin, and Asshur. They believe in omens and sorcery. They eat pork and other unclean animals. I have heard that they reek of strange spices. They are ignorant pagans—barbarians of the lowest order.

Even worse, the Assyrians once conquered Israel. They ruled our ancestors, treating them like dogs. They tried to force us Israelites to worship their gods; some Israelites intermarried with the Assyrians, contaminating our purity.

Not only was I horrified at the thought of going to Nineveh, I was afraid. I knew that the Lord has a soft heart when it comes to repentance. The Lord is gracious and merciful, and will forgive even the worst sins when there is genuine remorse. What if, by some wild chance, the Ninevites did repent? This repugnant thought made me shudder!

So I did the only sane thing: I fled in the opposite direction, to Tarshish. I soon learned that it's not easy to escape the Lord. As I was fleeing by ship, the Lord sent a great storm. I was below deck, sleeping. The captain roused me and cried, "Get up and pray to your god!" When I came up on deck, the boat was being slammed by giant waves. The sailors were decent men (for pagans, that is) and prayed to their gods, but to no avail. Desperate, they cast lots, and the lot fell upon me. I knew that I was the cause of the storm and told them I was fleeing from the Lord. I asked them to throw me overboard in order to abate God's wrath and save the ship, but the sailors were reluctant.

They rowed even harder and prayed—this time to the Lord—but the storm raged on. They didn't want to send me to my death, but finally they saw no other way to save themselves. Reluctantly, the sailors cast me overboard and into the jaws of the tempest.

What happened next is beyond imagining. I was swallowed whole by a giant sea-creature! I had escaped the depths of the sea, only to be faced now with a more unthinkable and bewildering end, being eaten alive by a colossal fish! I struggled for breath for the three days I was in the belly of this beast. I swam among the bile and stomach contents, unable to sleep. I had much time to think, and to pray. I begged the Lord for deliverance.

After the third day, I was vomited out of this monster onto the rocky shore. As I lay exhausted but grateful for light and air, the word of the Lord came to me again. Once more, the Lord said that I must go to Nineveh and proclaim his message. This time, I went.

Nineveh was a huge city, the largest I had ever seen. It took me an entire day to walk from the outskirts to the center market. There, among the merchants and shoppers, I began to proclaim the Lord's word: "In forty days, Nineveh will be destroyed if you do not repent and believe the Lord!" I repeated this over and over without passion. Because I cared nothing for the Ninevites, I was actually hoping to be ignored or even mocked.

The news of my preaching eventually reached the king of Nineveh. To my amazement, he immediately tore his robes, put on sackcloth, and sat in ashes. He wore these signs of repentance like a badge. Not only did he do this himself, he issued a decree for the entire city to follow his example! Soon, the whole city donned sackcloth and cried to the Lord for mercy.

I was appalled! The thought of these foreigners going through the motions of repentance revolted me. Couldn't the Lord see through this ruse? Didn't the Lord understand that the Ninevites were wearing sackcloth simply to escape destruction? Their so-called repentance was a travesty.

I cried out in distress, "O Lord, this is exactly what I feared. This is why I fled to Tarshish. For I knew that you were merciful and gracious, always ready to believe the best about humans, including Ninevites. O Lord, if you are not going to destroy Nineveh, then take my life from me!"

The Lord's response to my plea was simple: "Is it right for you to be angry?" I wanted to scream out to the Lord, My outrage is justified! The Ninevites deserved to be punished for their wickedness. Their repentance was a sham! The Lord was being blinded by his mercy.

In despair, I left Nineveh and made a shelter for myself on the side of a low hill overlooking the city. There, I waited and prayed for the destruction of the city. During the day, the sun was torrid. My shelter provided little shade; I was baking in it. The next morning, I awakened to a miracle. A castor bean plant had grown next to me, providing abundant cool shade. I was delighted with this lush, green shelter.

But when I awoke the very next day, the plant had withered. A cursed worm had destroyed my lovely shade bush! Just then, a wilting sirocco blew from the east, bringing oppressive heat. I became so faint, I prayed to the Lord for the relief of death.

Then the Lord spoke to me again, asking, "Is it right for you to be angry about the bush?"

I cried out through parched lips, "Yes, Lord, angry enough to die!" I hoped that the Lord would allow me to fade into eternal sleep. But the Lord had something else in mind for me.

The Lord said, "Jonah, you are so concerned about a bush that lived only one day, that you want to die. Shouldn't I be as concerned about Nineveh, a city where there are more than a hundred and twenty thousand persons who are ignorant of the way they should live?"

As I lay there hoping to die, something changed within me. Suddenly, I was ashamed of how I had acted and how I had spoken to the Lord. I had been arrogant and self-righteous. Even worse, I had been selfish and hateful. I wanted the Ninevites destroyed because they were foreigners, because they worshiped different gods and observed different customs.

I had another insight. I was jealous of the Lord's steadfast love. I wanted that love and mercy for my people only. I didn't want to share the Lord! I had ignored the third part of the Lord's covenant with our ancestor Abraham: that all the nations of the world would be blessed through Israel. Our faith in the one Lord is not a treasure to be hoarded, but a gift to share with the world.

I barely had the strength to drag myself into Nineveh. Seeing that I was near death, two Ninevites carried me to their home. After eating a piece of bread and drinking some water, I finally had the power to stand. I used my newfound strength to tear off my robe and put on sack-cloth. Then, I walked to the nearest ash heap and collapsed on it. With my remaining strength, I lifted my voice with the voices of the Ninevites, praying that the Lord would spare this city and its people.

Dear Lord, teach me to love all people, no matter what their race, nationality, or creed. Challenge me when I assume that differences cannot be bridged. Change my prejudices as you did Jonah's. In your holy name I pray. Amen.

Questions for Reflection and Discussion

• Why does Jonah initially refuse to speak God's word to the Ninevites? What prejudices does Jonah hold concerning Assyrians (Ninevites)? In what ways are you, or have you been, like Jonah?

• How is the Lord persistent with Jonah? What is Jonah's reaction to the Ninevites' repentance? Why does Jonah want to die in the desert? When have you begrudged God's mercy to another person?

• What lesson does God teach Jonah? Why is Jonah so blind to the third part of the covenant with Abraham? What does Jonah need to repent of? The book of Jonah ends with the Lord's indictment of Jonah. Do you think Jonah joined the Ninevites in repentance, as he does in the portrayal above, or do you believe he continued in his stubbornness?

Performing the Character Portrayals as Dramas

ONE POSSIBILITY FOR USING this book is to allow the characters to speak through you. These portrayals can be performed as dramatic monologues or dialogues in worship and classroom settings. For those who want to venture onto the stage or into the pulpit, here are some suggestions.

• Read the portrait aloud several times, trying to capture each character's voice. Walk in the character's shoes, imagining how the character would express himself or herself. If possible, deliver the portrait by memory.

• Decide whether to wear a costume or a simple robe to enhance the dramatic effect.

• For some characters, a prop can add to the dramatic effect. For example, you might hold a staff when portraying Moses or wear a queen's crown when portraying Esther. Be creative.

• When presenting "Jacob and Esau," you can perform it as a dialogue with two persons, or as a "one-person dialogue." If you choose the latter, you can distinguish between the characters by turning to one side when speaking as Jacob and to the other side when speaking as Esau. A variation on this technique can work for characters such as Abraham, as they move between past and present.

• Give a short introduction telling your audience that you are going to offer a dramatic monologue. "My name is [character's name]" is all that you will need most of the time.

• If you use a character portrayal as a sermon, decide whether or not you will sermonize about the character. If you do, the questions at the end of each chapter may suggest sermon directions.